MY LITTLE SPARTAN

Unleash Your Inner Spartan

Michael V Kalisperas

with
Elena and Ellie Kalisperas

ISBN 13: 978-1722966911

Table of Contents |

Prologue |

You know how life never seems to go right and all your un-imagined frustrations begin to come true, one after another?

Or when life had been giving you a fair deal, only for it to make a careening left turn and you find yourself in the middle of nowhere, wondering how on earth you got here?

Well, I would like to welcome you into our life, my wife Elena's, and mine. It's been about 5 years since Vasili was born, and although he's our lovely little son, we have struggled from one terrible experience to another and here I am, almost on the brink of a collapsed life.

Sometimes it seems as though our lives were planned from the beginning to head towards sorrow and to be soaked with grief, with no visible route of escape. However, there is a strong force deep within my soul that has never allowed me, or Elena, to give up.

Within the last 5 years, between Vasili and our third child Maria, we spent so much time in the hospital, it must be equivalent to months, that you wouldn't be wrong to call it our second home. All of that just seems wrong, so wrong yet, there's not much we can do about it. These days, I just seem so exasperated and worn out from the continuous stress of accepting what has happened to my son and having to accept that I cannot turn back time to make things right... if only!

It is challenging enough to watch him go through life in pain from severe brain damage, but to undergo so many additional surgeries and complications is a constant battle for him and for us. We can only give him all of our love and strength. We comfort him in the way we can to make his life as happy as can be. The joys he brings us when we see his beaming smile and twinkling eyes never fails to amaze me of his courage as the little boy that he is. We would do anything to help him, if only we could take his pain away.

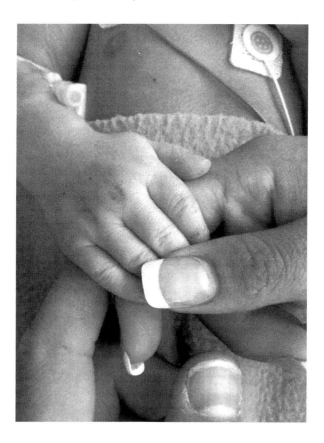

I am hopeful.

Hopeful, because I know there are others out there who may be experiencing the same life events and would probably feel as alone as we did. I would like this book to reach out to them, to serve as a comfort and a reminder that they are not alone in this challenge, and through sharing our story that they may find strength and remain strong in these trying times.

Hopeful, because I truly desire to be a source of light in this gloomy darkness, most especially for others all over the world who are facing the same challenges as I am, here.

Hopeful, because I want to share with you that sometimes it's okay to feel weak, it's okay to feel sad, it's okay to cry, it's okay when some days are better than others. More importantly, to help you understand that there will be slow days, days when you may not be as motivated to do all you can do for your disabled loved one. I need you to understand that it's okay to feel that way sometimes, it doesn't mean you don't love them enough or you are a bad parent, it just shows that you are human, and it's okay to be "human" sometimes.

The aim of this book is to help you to see laughter in the midst of the overwhelming pain and chaos, and to come out of such situations scarred but victorious, branded indeed, but with new layers of faith, hope and love which no one can ever remove.

As you read this book expect to experience, from the perspective of parents and siblings, the true effects that being disabled can have on both the affected ones and their care-givers. Prepare yourselves to read with great emotion the unabashed pages of Elena's diary and from the perspective of Vasili's young siblings, of living day to day in the world of disability and all that it brings to a family unit.

This book is majorly about my brave son, my little Spartan; Vasili Kalispera, the one who keeps teaching me life lessons through all of his challenges. And to him, it is dedicated.

I hope you find inspiration in it, and strength to overcome all of your troubles.

A Brief Note from Me |

It's important to find ways to get the balance with work or arrange with your partner ways to help each other. Obviously for me to grow and learn to work from home using marketing, affiliate marketing etc, meant it took time but its helped us all be together more.

I am offering help for any parent who is dealing with similar challenges talked about in this book.

Visit www.michaelkalisperas.com to get some free tools, advice and to contact me if you need to learn more about how to sustain your family financially during a time like this.

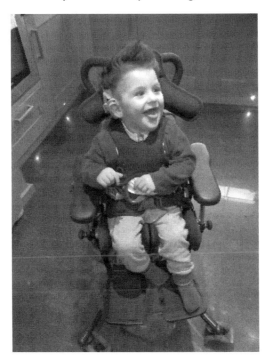

SECTION I:
THE UNRAVELLING

Chapter 1:

Of Birth: The Mingling of Joy and Pain |

It was May 2012, my wife, young and full of life, had been overexcited throughout this particular pregnancy as opposed to that of our first child. For this, I was a thankful husband. You do not want to know how miserable I got before the birth of our first child, and this was influenced by my wife's incessant bouts of depression. She would be happy one minute, yet sad the next; so rapid were her mood swings, that I was almost always at a loss on what to do to make her happy. I could do something that made her happy one minute. Then the next, that same thing would only cause her to become sad. I practically walked on egg shells around her during that period.

But fortunately, it wasn't the same, this time with Vasili. During Vasili's pregnancy, my wife was almost too cheerful. And thinking about it now, a sad smile tugs at the corners of my lips. Whenever I remember how excitedly she had picked out her outfits each day, the sheer glow on her face whenever she felt him move, and all those perky little things that made carrying a child so beautiful, I just smile. She truly bloomed throughout the nine months.

It was indeed, with fervour, that she had schooled our 3-year-old daughter on what was 'inside mommy's tummy' and what it meant to be an elder sibling. I wouldn't be wrong if I said she convinced our little girl to believe having a younger one was the ultimate bliss, it was almost akin to rapture. She told her tales of how wonderful it would be to have someone to play with every single day and how she wouldn't have to ride her bicycle alone or play with her toys on her own. As expected, soon enough, my baby girl was enthusiastically marking the calendar and every day, counting down to Vasili's birth.

Vasili

Vasili means King. My son is a king, by virtue of him being mine in the first place and also because I planned to train him to see a king within himself and to project kingship at every step of the way in his life. Little did I know, that my naming him Vasili was only because in him, came complete royalty. Over and over again, he has demonstrated to me how a king should act even in the face of pain and perceived helplessness! Looking back, I wish we could pause those moments between Elena and me, replay them with me hanging onto Elena's laughter, every last loud giggle. Also how she would continuously bug me with silly complaints, which at that time had sounded silly but now, they sound like forlorn privileges, gone and never to be recovered.

Vasili was born about 10 days after his expected due date. At his birth, he was absolutely breath-taking and there just aren't enough words to describe how magical he looked. I absolutely adored him and bonded immediately, as did everyone else present at his birth. Now when I think about it in retrospect, he was such a beautiful child that anyone who came in contact with him couldn't help but adore him. Such was his charm. My wife had an amazing water birth and as soon as she gave birth, she emerged from the water trembling, her body still in shock from a natural birth. The midwife came to check on her and said she was fine and good to go but Elena pleaded to stay the night, so she could rest and also spend some quality time with our newborn son before we would head home. Consequently, we were sent to room 13, a dark room, where she would stay the night and I then headed home to spread the news as I allowed the two of them to bond. Only after a few hours of being away, I was already missing them and not being able to bear it any longer, I went back to the hospital that evening, as a proud dad all over again. We bonded as a family as I keenly watched over my wife as she breastfed our son. We were both ecstatic at how alert he was the entire period. This gave us immense joy and satisfaction of doing the best for our baby boy. Since my wife had been an expert at breast feeding our daughter, she was proud that our son was latching on quite quickly too. In our state of happiness, we felt it would be best to return home that night, deciding against being discharged in the early morning. We informed the nurse of our decision and she in turn requested a paediatrician to review us before we could be discharged.

My wife has never forgotten the moment that we arrived home, as even now, she hasn't stopped talking about it. When she took Vasili upstairs to Ellie's (our eldest daughter) bedroom she said, 'Your brother is home!' She hardly believed that call as she had been waiting so long and he was already overdue. Elena spoke out again but because Ellie was still very much asleep, she kept on tossing and turning in her bed until Vasili made a sound. She instantly roused and jumped up with a beaming smile and fell in love with him at first sight. Elena looked like a million dollars, you could feel her pride and happiness radiating from her face, and this was easily the happiest moment of her life up until now. She had never felt so content to finally have her two children safe at home.

That night Vasili and Elena didn't get much sleep as Elena had to keep on breastfeeding on demand a very active Vasili throughout the night.

The next day, during the very early hours of the morning, we noticed that he looked quite yellow. However, since Ellie had also been very yellow as a baby, we didn't really think much of it at that time. Throughout the day we had different family members pay us visits in order to felicitate with us and meet our newborn son. My mother was the first of them and it was midday when she arrived. Taking a comfortable position in the kitchen, she then sat with Elena's mum who had also come to visit and was cradling Vasili, a look of complete adoration plastered over her face as they both doted over their little grandson. Eventually, after much scrutiny, they both agreed that he was quite yellow- jaundiced.

Elena was unbelievably energetic considering that she had just given birth; she was in fact, on cloud nine. The midwife arrived, a lovely middle-aged woman, who was not in uniform. Elena went to the door with Vasili and they sat in the lounge away from too much noise. Elena held Vasili in her arms the whole time as they discussed Elena's maternity notes and had a casual chat about our Greek background and some other small talk. Elena expressed her deep-seated concerns about his jaundice and her fear of not having enough milk, but the midwife reassured Elena that jaundice was quite normal and that just by putting him close to the window, he would be fine. In response Elena pointed out that there was no sunshine since the weather was very overcast. Either way, Elena took her advice and spent the rest of the day in the conservatory trying to get him as close to the window as possible. She was also reassured that her milk wouldn't start flowing until after the third day following the birth but regardless of that, she should carry on breastfeeding. The midwife didn't look thoroughly at Vasili to visually judge his jaundice, nor did she attempt to carry out any confirmatory tests or suggest we visit the hospital to do so. I can also remember my mum going over to where Elena and the midwife were seated before she left. She greeted the midwife and politely asked if she would like a drink, in that time she also expressed her concerns regarding Vasili and his present condition but our worries were laid to rest by the midwife. She reassured us and continued to do so until she left, saying that all was okay and that he only needed exposure to sunlight and he would be fine.

That evening, Elena and her mum gave Vasili his first bath, followed by an unsettled night during which our little boy cried and cried. Elena tried hard to settle him and persist in breastfeeding. Elena's mum had continually asked if all was okay, but we said confidently that we would cope. Elena decided to try feeding him some formula, if that would quiet him as she thought that maybe she just didn't have enough milk to feed his hunger. After he had taken some formula, he finally fell asleep around 5 am. That morning, he was much more content. He slept a lot and didn't drink so much, so we assumed that he had finally filled up his tummy. We waited for my family to visit again for lunch and my mum expressed her concerns once again at how yellow he was, and she kept asking us, over and over again about what the midwife said. We let her know that we had been reassured, told to stay close to the window and to keep on feeding him.

I still remember this conversation so vividly because it seemed like the last 'almost normal' conversation we had before everything changed forever. At this point, Vasili was still asleep in the conservatory. Elena had gone over to his little Moses basket to rouse him, change his nappy and feed him since he hadn't woken up for a feed. It was with sheer horror as she assessed that his head seemed floppy, and when she wanted to change his nappy, she noticed that the colour of his wee came out as orange. In that instant, alarm bells were ringing in Elena's head and when I came over to where she was, since she was taking too long, she was talking on the phone with the midwife whom she had called straight away, to express her concerns about the fear that something was not right.

A different midwife arrived and together, she and Elena went to take a look at Vasili. After her examination of the young lad, she proceeded to say that he'd definitely been 'tangoed'. I must admit I was taken back by this comment as I only knew the word 'tangoed' from a television advertisement about an orange flavoured fizzy drink. I was at a loss as to what she meant by it in this circumstance and would only discover with horror at a later point.

She called the hospital to send us for a review and told us to take him in to be further looked at but there was no urgency in her voice. I think it was the professional in her keeping calm. At this point however, irrespective of what her recommendation was, we had already decided in favour of going to the hospital, and were ready to drive straight down there. We took him the moment she left, and had to once again, say our goodbyes to our beloved Ellie; feeling that it was unfair and pretty hard to leave her once again but she had to stay with my family at home.

In a short time, we arrived at the hospital and as soon as we got there, we were asked for our purple notes. We hadn't thought to bring them in our panic, so we called my father to bring them over to the hospital while we waited. As we waited to be sent into a treatment room, I went out to collect the purple notes from my father whom I could see parking his car. Unknown to me, at about the same time as I headed out to collect the notes from my father, the doctor spoke to my wife and she was told that Vasili would need phototherapy as well as a double exchange blood transfusion. On my return, I couldn't help but notice the fear in Elena's eyes and I asked what she had been told. After she had relayed the doctor's message to me, her fear immediately transferred on to me. I really do not like seeing those pretty eyes of hers disturbed. And even whilst we were waiting in a room at the hospital, in what seemed an agonising wait, Vasili's skin was increasingly and evidently turning a pale orange colour, which alarmed us further and we immediately rushed to ask the doctor to hurry, if only to get some re-assurance that all was or would be, well.

The mere fact that we were expected to travel back to collect the baby notes and were left in a waiting room, and to worsen matters the tangoed comment, made the situation seem not as urgent as what the fear in our hearts and what our parental instinct were telling us. Nevertheless, we had to play by their rules, as you cannot simply pick a room and expect to be seen instantly by a doctor. However, Elena, my rock, knew that something was not right; how she knew, I can't say but I can only guess that maybe it was her maternal instinct that was telling her so. For me I had a deep hope that all would be okay. To me it was jaundice and many kids have jaundice, right? Well yes and no. There are two types, pathological jaundice and physiological jaundice.

Before proceeding any further, I feel I should bring you to an understanding of the condition called Jaundice. Before Vasili, I had almost paid no attention to it, but in trying to understand what he was going through and how I could help, I have been able to tutor myself to some extent on his condition. It is my sincere hope, like I have earlier said, that this book serves as a point of reference for all those who may be going through a similar challenge. What good does it do, if it doesn't inform or educate?

Jaundice or Hyperbilirubinemia

Hyperbilirubinemia, or jaundice, is a life-threatening disorder in newborns. It is a multifactorial disorder with many symptoms. Generally, the physiological jaundice is the more prevalent type. However, in some parts of the world, pathological jaundice is also common. Jaundice is easily diagnosable. However, it requires a quick and on the spot treatment and, if it's not treated properly, it can lead to many and very severe complications and sometimes, death. Currently the treatment options for jaundice are basically phototherapy, chemotherapy, and vaccinations. Jaundice can affect children and adults alike, but it is more prevalent in children. One of the most prevalent clinical conditions for hyperbilirubinemia is the Neonatal hyperbilirubinemia, which is a common clinical problem encountered during the neonatal period, especially in the first week of life.

Neonatal jaundice is the discolouration of the skin and sclera (the white portion of the eyes) to a yellowish colour in a newborn, which is caused by the presence of bilirubin. These phenomena can create a grave concern in the doctor and medical staff as well as anxiety in the parents.

There are several types of Bilirubinemia that have been reported in infants (neonates) and it includes physiological jaundice, pathological jaundice, jaundice due to breastfeeding or breast milk and haemolytic jaundice including three subtypes due to Rh factor incompatibility, ABO blood group incompatibility and Jaundice associated with Glucose-6-phosphate dehydrogenase (G6PD) deficiency. For the purpose of this book, I will only consider psychological and pathological hyperbilirubinemia or jaundice as it's commonly known.

Psychological Jaundice

This is the most common type of new-born hyperbilirubinemia. For children who have suffered from this type of Jaundice, there is the likelihood of developing neurodevelopmental abnormalities which includes athetosis, loss of hearing, and in some rare cases, intellectual deficits. These are caused by the high toxic level of bilirubin in the infant's blood. Jaundice attributable to physiological immaturity would usually appear between 24–72hrs of age and would peak at between the 4th and 5th days in term neonates and for preterm, at the 7th day. If managed properly, it should disappear by the 10th – 14th day of life. Unconjugated bilirubin is the predominant form and usually has its serum level at less than 15 mg/dl.

Pathological Jaundice

Bilirubin levels with a deviation from the normal range and requiring immediate intervention would be described as pathological jaundice. Appearance of jaundice within 24hrs due to increase in serum bilirubin beyond 5 mg/dl/day, peak levels higher than the expected normal range, presence of clinical jaundice more than 2 weeks and conjugated bilirubin (dark yellowish urine staining the clothes) are categorised under this type of jaundice. This is the sort that needs immediate treatment and for which National Institute of Clinical Excellence (NICE) guidelines are already in place. The proper treatment for this type of Jaundice is phototherapy and blood transfusion.

To find out that a simple blood test, the cost of just one pound (US $1.32), would have prevented all the troubles and sleepless nights that we have had to go through, never mind the permanent damage it caused. To think that it is an integral part of patient care guidelines, makes me question further what the healthcare providers were thinking of and whose responsibility it was to notice these things.

The level at which jaundice can be said to be dangerous is measured by the level of bilirubin in the blood and, like I earlier mentioned, in our son's case this is what eventually scarred his brain. The level of bilirubin in his blood was way above the normal range and it led to the toxicity and scarring of his brain tissues. The problem wasn't a question of which guidelines to follow, but more about the fact that these guidelines were not followed at all. I truly was not aware of the magnitude of the missed opportunities for preventive actions, actions which weren't carried out, as well as some shocking news of negligence; mistakes that eventually became clear during further investigation.

To me it was merely the yellowing of the skin, which I knew happened with many babies, because I was not a trained medical professional. I am merely a layman, what do I know about medicine and neonatal childcare? The people we trusted with our precious baby were trained however, and in spite of that training, this still had to occur. We forgave the health service very early after we realised that holding any anger towards them was not going to solve anything. To many it was almost impossible to believe that we could forgive such a grave hurt, but we had to move on as best as we could, and this was one decision closer to acceptance. I was merely being optimistic and thinking we would be back home as a family soon enough and all would be well.

But that was not to be the case. All wasn't even close to being well; not by a far mile.

We were asked to sit and wait outside the glass windowed room as we saw the doctors attempting to place my fidgety but increasingly lethargic son into an incubator style box, I presumed, for phototherapy. What I experienced next has been etched in my memory for life, the pain of witnessing such events staining my brain, quite similar to the way bilirubin stained my own son's brain causing so much damage. The after effect was so severe, much stronger than a bolt of electric current through my veins that my wife and I needed to attend PTSD therapy sessions including EMDR treatment to help overcome the sudden shock and the intense swift emotional contrast of happiness to deep sadness. One moment we were blessed with the arrival of our beautiful son, and the next, it quickly become the most traumatic event you could imagine.

As a matter of fact, having to pen down some parts of this book has taken all the courage I can manage to muster at times. I have learnt to accept these bad memories, as focusing so much of my energy on them can really do nothing positive, nothing except to draw me back into such a negative state that is non-productive for me or for my family. With the help of professionals and my own self teachings, I have been able to forgive and move on.

Receiving psychological help for my wife and later on, for myself, has been a challenge in itself. With the early years of adapting to our circumstance and the miscommunications between professionals at great expense to our health, is another story in itself. I would say that our mental health institutions desperately need far more resources and funding and had we not been financially saving as individuals and as a family, we wouldn't have been able to afford some of the services or even cope. Just thinking about it, I cannot begin to imagine the outcome of not finding our own Spartans Within!

The very day Vasili was admitted, as the doctors, nurses and other members of the health care team worked in a hurried frenzy, all I could do was look on in wide-eyed shock, somewhat lost yet very present. None of it felt real, it was almost as though I was an observer looking in.

The next three months went by in a blur and daily, each member of my family slipped more and more into a blurry sense of existence. We literally stopped living because, day in and day out, we seemed to be on a constant vigil for Vasili. Those early years we had no support from anyone and it was extremely difficult to see a way forward and sometimes we felt so alone even in the midst of the crowd and activities that existed around us.

To worsen our anxiety, we were not informed about what was happening with our son. In fact, it seemed to me, with every passing day, that critical information was being specifically withheld from us and that the medical staff spoke in hushed tones around us. This could possibly have been my paranoia but nevertheless, I took it upon myself to record every bit of information and paperwork which I came in contact with, as a way to source for help from a medical specialist negligence team later on.

We were increasingly scared with each passing day. Was it something we had done? Was it something we had not done? Self-blame crippled our thoughts and guilt was etched in our minds as parents. We hadn't had this problem with our first born so it made it even harder to relate with. We paced across the hall, and every minute we watched to see if the baby in the intensive care unit being managed was our child or another for there were other babies there, too. We hugged, cried, raked our hands through our hair, stood, wrung our hands, and then we did nothing. The motions became cyclic and after a while, we couldn't simply go through any of those motions again, it was like we began to steel our minds expecting the worst and refuting it all at the same time.

His birth had been normal, there hadn't been a caesarean section, and he was discharged to go home shortly after having been inspected and confirmed to be healthy. So what was this issue that had arisen? Why was it so close to his birth and if it was a problem from birth, why hadn't it been noticed before he was discharged to go home? Why had that first midwife handled the situation like it was nothing to be worried about, and yet the medical staff here was acting in such a frenzy to keep him in good health once we got to the ward? These and many more questions ran through our minds relentlessly at a sped up rate.

As soon as they heard that there seemed to be a problem, my brother and sister came to see us, and soon enough we were surrounded by other family members who had come around because of his birth and were now with us in the hospital family waiting room with the feelings of helplessness and sorrow etched all over their faces. No one deserved this, to be basking in the celebration of the birth of a child, only to have that abruptly taken away by a yet unnamed illness. It might have been unnamed, but it was later obvious to all, that it was pretty severe and life threatening.

Later that evening, we were addressed by the doctor and told the most shocking news of our lives. Our son had been born healthy and that was not being questioned. However, there had been an oversight, a common one – actually it was that his bilirubin level had not been measured, and so it had been missed that he had high levels of this metabolite, causing it to become toxic in his body, and it hadn't stopped at that, but the metabolite had continually accumulated in his brain, resulting into severe brain damage.

Some parts of his brain had been damaged by bilirubin; a condition known as, KERNICTERUS. Over the next few months and years even, we would become more familiar with this disabling illness, as well as other associated conditions because we were going to have to deal with a lot. I could tell by the look on the faces of the doctors and nurses who were attending to him that this was going to be our fate and indeed for a long time.

KERNICTERUS - is a very rare type of brain damage that occurs in a newborn with severe jaundice. It happens when the metabolite bilirubin in the blood builds up to very high levels and spreads into the brain tissue causing permanent brain damage. But note this: it can be prevented if the causative condition, which is jaundice, is detected and treated early enough before it causes any damage.

The effect of the deposition of bilirubin in certain crucial areas of his brain meant that he had also developed Cerebral Palsy as just one of the results, and from where we stood, I could see that my son's legs were crossed. He followed my eyes and the consultant told me sadly, that he may never walk and that if he did, it would be with mostly a scissor gait, but that there were options for his management; specific types of physiotherapy were strongly suggested to try.

For now, we just had to get him out of the critical state in which he was in. As we watched on, we saw our son have a series of seizures even as the nurses were holding him and trying to medicate him, he still kept on having these seizures with his entire little body contorting and his back arching, as well as some very abnormal eye and muscle movements.

For a long time afterwards, we remained in utter shock. We couldn't believe what we were hearing, yet we had so many questions. Somehow, we had gone from 'happily ever after', to the 'sad story begins'; all within the blink of an eye. There was no debating it, our lives had truly changed, forever.

Throughout the weeks during which Vasili was admitted at the hospital, and after we had been told about the diagnosis, there was one really sad thing that kept bugging me, that feeling of hopelessness and the fact that we were left to ourselves to seemingly figure things out on our own with almost no counselling. This was indeed devastating for us and traumatising for my wife, my daughter, myself; and us all. Yet, we were compelled to try as much as possible to stay as strong as we could for our daughter; for indeed, it was very painful for our first daughter to watch her mother cry so constantly as well as to watch my face stay pale and staunch for prolonged periods. She needed a strong parent around her to help her to cope also.

I was the man. I had been taught in my childhood, in an implied and passive sense rather than actively, that in such circumstances you don't show fear, instead you maintain this strong mien and carry on with super-strength for your family, but I didn't know for how long (and truly it didn't take long before I broke down) I could maintain this facade and live this lie I was beginning to live, albeit with a lot of effort. The strain felt unbearable.

Surrounded by so much pain and uncertainty, I had written a letter to the doctors and as I read it out loud to my family, they all wept, as if we all were grieving the loss of my son together in a crowded circle. The priest came to give a blessing, and we mourned as though it was his funeral. We prayed that he would keep strong and stay alive every single day. We prayed and begged for such faith and hope as would be required for him to make it through. We had to wait for him to come off of support slowly, and I was constantly on edge to know if he would make it every day, every hour, every minute and every second, living in the fight or flight state continually. The first time we held him in our arms again, we felt a little bit of satisfaction and some relief. Elena had been so desperate to hold him again, and as she carried him in her arms, I watched on as she wept and cleaned his dry lips. As she did so, the nurse took photos; just in case that would be our last chance to hold him in our arms. At every juncture, only spaced by a few minutes and sometimes, even seconds, the alarm would go off and scare us every time his oxygen levels had dropped too low. At times, we just didn't know if he was ever going to make it, and we stayed by his side each day until later when he was out of the ventilator. He looked a pale green colour from so much phototherapy. I particularly resented the fact that no one seemed to be talking to us, I felt we were invisible. Had we become such a nuisance? Or were we simply considered so unimportant that we didn't need to be talked to? Apart from that doctor who addressed us, we got very little information from the medical staff and indeed still today, most of what we know about Vasili's condition, we have had to research ourselves, or have learned from the support groups to which we belong. Even after it was revealed that there was a problem with our child, we were not given much information as to whether something could be done to improve his condition, or to prevent the effects from becoming more severe.

Does this speak volumes about the training of our medical personnel or is it simply a result of a lack of communication skills, or even because they are overworked and have little to no time? I would truly love to get a response to that, if possible, but if I would hazard a guess, it would be that it was a contribution from all three factors more than it is a function of one.

If I had the chance, I would love to speak directly to the NHS about some of these matters, and especially about medical education in our country. I have been doing a little of this on social media platforms, but, well, I'm not influential enough on social media to get such rapt attention from the NHS. Don't get me wrong, my speaking at the Patient Safety Lead after writing to the government was helpful but it's still not enough. There always seems to be a failing in moving towards any proactive and meaningful change. That being said, I can only be forever grateful for the neonatal team for saving my son's life.

Sadly, I had even gathered along the way that the first midwife that visited us had been a student who wasn't accompanied by a supervisor or mentor, and that she really was not experienced or knowledgeable enough to have said that my child was fine, just like that. In addition, I have read several articles which have proven that negligence by maternity staff have resulted in several problems with birth, not just my son's, but that of a lot of other children in the world. I wonder how many of such children have died, their little bodies not being able to cope and how many more have been rendered disabled. I understand that mistakes happen and when they do, that we are at the receiving end, but certain mistakes are deemed in the medical world by a term called a "never event" as there are guidelines in place to prevent them from occurring. In effect, they are so preventable that it is a serious concern if they do occur.

During such a difficult time in my life I am so glad I've had my wife Elena beside me. I asked her to contribute to my autobiography in her own words as she has been my rock beside me throughout this journey and would like to share her experiences from a wife and mother's perspective....

Elena's Diary

I will never forget the out of body experience, it was so surreal! My family and I all surrounding Vasili's cot bed in the neonatal ward while I watched myself like a picture hoping that one day I could look back on this day and tell him what had happened like a story and how everything was all going to be okay.

A mother's bond is so immense and unbreakable.

It's amazing how much you can say with no words spoken.

I would hold Vasili so tight and cry that I thought he could no longer hear my heart beat, but I was encouraged by a speech and language therapist that he could feel the vibration of my heart, he could feel my every move, my pulse, my breath, skin to skin and nose to nose.

He would hold my neck whilst I sang to him so he could feel the vibrations of my voice and we would dance all night long just to see his beaming smile and hear his belly laugh!

I could barely see him through all the tubes in the intensive care unit fighting for his life, contorting his body. I felt hopeless!

I was living a real-life nightmare, I couldn't think of anything worse. I have never cried so much and it's true what they say, I cried a river! I cried until my tears ran dry! I slowly became numb. It took months of constant trauma; revealing he was blind, revealing he was deaf, revealing he had cerebral palsy all in result to jaundice. I was kicking myself. Why didn't I know? Why are parents not made aware about the dangers of jaundice if it's so common in children? Why wasn't I given any signs to look out for? Why was there no follow up advice or check up? I was angry, devastated, sleep deprived, depressed, traumatised all at the same time. It was a whole new world of appointments every day I just didn't know how I was going to get through a day never mind a week!

There is no doubt that my heart had been shattered into a million pieces and I'm slowly putting some of the pieces back together again but as you know once you try to mend something which is broken it's never quite the same, there will always be a big piece missing.

I will always worry for now and the future.

The what if's will haunt me, the flash backs will always replay but my coping mechanism has been to focus on each day and to live in the moment. I do the best that I can do for my family and all that matters to me is to see the smile on my children's faces.

Chapter 2:
That September

That September, having almost gotten used to the fact that we could not wish away Vasili's Kernicterus state, we began to do the only thing we really could, which was to accept it. What didn't we do? Cry? Pray? Blame the hospital? Question the reason for this incidence?

Eventually, the truth began to sink in, that it was for real, and it was not going away.

I tried finding that sparkle in my boy's eyes. Endlessly I waited and boy, did I try, but I couldn't.

Every morning, I woke up from my few hours of true sleep. Persistently low-spirited, absolutely unable to think of anything uplifting, and with bags always beneath my eyes.

I had suffered from depression in the past, had taken medications and gone for counselling and supposedly, I had gotten over it. But that September was about to set me spiralling down a black hole that was endless. Now, I simply lived in a surreal and darkened place and was still unable to fully grasp the full meaning of what had befallen my family and me. I hadn't come to terms with it, and for the next 4 months, I still wasn't able to come to terms with it, walking around like I was in a trance, looking at an image which resembled my son but wasn't quite

23

my son and walking away wishing it was all a dream that I would soon awaken from. It wasn't, and there was no escaping this. It was our life and I just had to get used to it, and although I had started to come to accept this, I still didn't find the strength to believe it was true or that we could survive this. My mind felt as though it was playing tricks on me.

But another event was about to happen. One which would finally tip me into the deep depression which I was already on the brink of.

I still remember the date very clearly; it was around 8pm on the 25th of September and I was driving back home from the local supermarket where I had gone to get a few things for the family's use. I really cannot say how or why it had happened, but I presume the other driver was not concentrating and coupled with my low energy, I couldn't even swerve off of the road in time and we ended up in a terrible car crash, with both cars smashed up. In fact, this was a description that matched my state of mind quite aptly also.

Luckily, we had both survived and after the driver had mumbled a slight 'Sorry', she randomly walked off. I was too weak to challenge this, and as she walked, I wondered if I too, could walk away in that same way; walk away from all this mess that my life had turned into, walk away and move far away to some remote suburb where I could start living my life afresh.

I jolted myself back to the scene of the accident and my reality. As I sat in the parking lot looking at the police officers who arrived to the scene of the car-crash, I contemplated my new life and tears started to fall from my face. I had no clear mind, and now, I had no car.

I hitched a lift with a stranger who had driven pass and witnessed the mess. Back home everyone stared blankly at one another, these days, a strange normalcy of just getting by with lack of sleep and shock mixed in one sorry heap of a drained human existence.

Some friends and family were kind enough to drop by and bring us food, and we found this a comfort as cooking was not at the forefront of our minds. Although it felt shameful at first, we soon got used to the routine and started appreciating the help. Now, it meant one less meal to be cooked, one less worry for my wife and me, but my wife especially. It cut me so deep that I couldn't do much to help her more, and this made me sink even more into depression.

But that crash in September was the height of all that I could take. I couldn't take it anymore. I'd reached my breaking point. My car was written off and I felt like a total failure, one who could really offer no value to anyone, at least not anymore. I felt like l had failed my family, my wife and daughter especially. It turned out that we weren't really doing our daughter any favours, all we'd done was to place an additional burden on her young shoulders and expected her to carry those heavy burdens of saddened adulthood. We held a lot of information back from her, and although she was only four years old, she was not stupid, she knew everything, she could sense the pain and see the hurt in our eyes and in the way we acted around the house. There was only so much you could keep hidden in an attempt to protect her going forwards.

It started slowly: I began to overeat. At first, it was a little bit of everything I craved, and then I began to stay mostly in my room. Having hired a solicitor to oversee the affairs, it allowed me time to be on my own. Seeing as my overeating habits annoyed my wife and she almost wanted nothing to do with me, it seemed better that way. In spite of that, I still ate and continued to binge on comfort foods.

I overate so much that I began to put on a lot of weight in a short space of time. As a result of rapidly gaining weight, I now stayed strictly indoors, and was obviously in a hateful relationship with my body. I could barely look myself in the mirror and I could feel disgust seeping out of every pore in my body and more, because I knew that I was no longer the man I used to be. The man I was at this point, bore no resemblance to the man I'd been only about a year and a half ago. The turn of events had been drastic, almost incomprehensible, and the fact that I felt nothing could be done about it made it even worse, almost driving me to insanity.

And then people I knew, my brother who also doubled as my business partner (yes, I once had a business but that I will get into later), my parents, and even my wife, were concerned about my weight to the extent that they suggested that I have a form of weight loss surgery. My Body Mass Index was now well over 40, nearing 45 and clearly within the range of morbid obesity. It was my idea at first, but I needed some support and then realised I needed to do something about it and to do it fast. Coupled with depression, I had no other way out of my obese state aside from surgery. On consultations with the doctors, they welcomed the idea and they even believed it would lift me out of the depression since the obesity was now contributing significantly to my depressed state. I was in a complete fix.

To do, or not to do?

The next few days were tumultuous for me because I had buried my mind beneath this pile of flesh I now possessed and had almost forgotten what it meant to think clearly or to make a valid decision.

I had aged, but not necessarily grown wiser by all of these incidents, instead, my mind felt numb. I gave into the pressure of my thoughts and was briefed about the procedure to be performed, it was called a gastric sleeve. I watched on with mild amusement as the surgeon described the procedure to me, a significant portion of my stomach would be removed and this was going to severely limit the amount of food I could consume. Well, I acquiesced, and the surgery was performed. I lost a lot of weight in a short space of time and I was able to regain some of my energy back.

Still, I remained depressed. Slowly but surely, I began to accumulate all of the weight lost because I just wouldn't stop eating regardless of the fact that my stomach size had been reduced significantly. I kept eating mindlessly, not really caring, and my stomach kept on expanding, almost leading to a catastrophic state, I was later told by my doctors.

Somewhere beneath all of these depressed layers of my heart, light still managed to shine a little. I didn't feel totally broken because I felt that my story could help others live through painful periods and come out victorious, beating their pain hands down, again and again! That thought gave me some strength that I grasped onto and did not let go of.

When I slowly began to regain a sense of this light, I started to reach out to my wife and to try to rebuild what had now become a severely strained relationship.

She had been going through her own issues, but I hadn't been there to help as much as I ought to or would have wanted in more normal circumstances. If only I could do it all and let her rest and come to terms with it all.

Besides my obesity, I had also been dealing with a lot of other medical conditions which later reared their ugly effects, including the deficiencies of Vitamins B12, C and D. And all of these were in addition to my depression. I was taking injections for the B12 deficiency, and stopped taking them after a few years, only to have severe pains all over my body. I discovered that it was due to this same issue which I thought had been fully resolved, but apparently not. Just to add to the batch of pains, I also had a painful but common foot condition called Plantar Fasciitis, which gives an infected person the feeling of walking on nails. Not pleasant.

One thing I have learnt though, through all of these incredibly difficult experiences, is the building of a quiet form of inner strength, of resilience, the knowledge that even surviving through another day was indeed a miracle and worthy of celebration which is what I do now.

Chapter 3:
My Work Life: Past, Present and Future |

The Purpose in My Pain

It might be a little difficult to believe that I had once worked for the BBC and in London, as one of their notable designers. I had also moved on to set up my own freelance company. Seeing how my life was turning out, I wish sometimes that I had stayed back and not made some of the decisions I made. I could have gotten a little more experience, simply stayed away from all of the problems trailing me, but I didn't. Hindsight can be a painful thing.

I had come back home because my family needed help in the family business and I had this brilliant idea of setting up my own company. I had always itched to have a business of my own and when this opportunity presented itself in my mind, I couldn't ignore it. I just couldn't resist the lure.

I packed my bags, said goodbye to the British Broadcasting Corporation and, in extension, to all of the lovely friends I had acquired in London and headed back home. I had spent 5 years in London, and I would sorely miss London. How sorely though, I didn't know at the time.

The years flew by. I was working tirelessly to set up my new design company and ensuring that it was innovative enough to be a household name. I helped run my family's takeaway business part of the week, helping my brother and father and in my spare time I would fix up my own property slowly over the years.

I eventually met my beautiful wife a few years after moving back home and had married her in the summer a couple of years later. They say that when you meet the girl who is the One, you are certain that you do not want to lose her, so you are very quick to make everyone know that she is yours by marrying her, which is exactly what I did.

After marriage, I didn't lose concentration at work, but a new sense of responsibility began to dawn on me. My brother had always been the responsible one, always at home and always ready to take care of family business. I, the dyslexic and always the ill one as a child, had wanted to see a little more of the world and this is what had led me in the direction of London to see for myself, the beauty of that place. I wasn't wrong, for London was indeed a beautiful city.

When my wife became pregnant a few months into our marriage, my sense of responsibility grew even more. I was in love with her, and also in love with the idea of starting a family. It shone on my face, my immense desire to be a good man, to take care of my family and I directed this energy towards building our company into a very enviable and reputable one, indeed.

That first pregnancy was pretty challenging. And being our first, it took a lot of adjusting for us to get a hang of how to handle this new life we now lived. I remember that my wife was in a particularly sour mood almost all of the time, and this fuelled my desire to help her at home and relieve her of any discomfort which she might be feeling. However, I silently prayed that she would deliver our baby on time so she could go back to being the friendly, loving woman I had married. She is going to kill me when she reads this!

Our first child was a girl. A beautiful girl we named Ellie whom we certainly loved and adored, me especially. I was present for her birth. I had initially been in the birthing room where her mother had been groaning and shouting, but I couldn't bear it anymore. When the nursing staff saw how close I was to tears, they reassured me after they noticed I was in a constant infinite loop of pacing back and forth, in silence, each cry jabbing at my heart like a dagger. The torture was only to come to end with great relief when the nurse had congratulated me heartily saying: "it's a girl".

It was over, in a blur I rushed to hug my now calmly smiling wife who held our baby in her hands. We would later name her Ellie. I absolutely went mad over her surreal beauty the moment I set my eyes on her. She would become daddy's girl, the one I would always love and this I knew from the very moment she appeared into our lives. I would let no evil come to her as long as I was alive.

Over the next 2 years, I maintained a certain glow, that renewed glow of a new father who was both proud of himself and his new achievement of fathering a child, as indeed, I was. Only a handful of people wouldn't have noticed that I was so very happy. It showed on my face, and in everything I did. I walked like a king, talked like a king, moved like a king, attended to customers like they were kings, I was floating on cloud nine.

Sometimes, when I feel depressed, I take my mind back to those days, wishing I could hold on tightly to the days when I was as free of sorrow as I could have been, and then I am almost tempted to cry out in pain and anguish as regards to how bad my life had turned out. I was in a mess indeed.

Every day, after work, I would stop at the local store or the ice cream stand to buy something nice which I could take home for both my queens, and on getting home I would play so much with my daughter and she would laugh so hard that after everything, she would end up sleeping in my arms.

Just a little over two years after the birth of our daughter, we planned to have another child because my wife had always wanted a large family. Hence, Vasili's pregnancy.

Like I have alluded to earlier, this was much easier for my wife to handle than our daughter's. It was so easy that it got me a little worried. She had little to no experience of morning sickness, and was up and about doing every little thing she loved to do with so much precision, it scared me to my bones. Where was she getting all of this strength from?

I had expected that with this new pregnancy, I would lose a little of my wife. I would be subjected to an errand boy and be ready to obey her every whim and command. I was definitely a fool for love, but it didn't disturb me, because here before me was the love of my life and there was absolutely no excuse for her to be in pain.

But this pregnancy had been utterly free of stress and I was tempted to think in the months and years which followed that maybe, just maybe, it could be, that the freedom we had experienced during our previous existence was nature's means of placating us for the incomparable sorrow to come, for the stabbing pain that went through my heart each time he was unwell and for each time he had to be rushed into hospital.

After he was born and diagnosed with Kernicterus, life became challenging not just for him, but for everyone at home. Of course, after the first few months of literally living within the hospital premises because we simply had to, we were discharged to go home and to come only for follow up visits.

To calm my depression a little, I decided to go back to work. I had to, I had to earn a living and I also felt it may help me move to into a position of normalising this whirlwind of an existence.

But on my return to work, I couldn't bring myself to find the energy to work, concentrate, and then to also cope with all the questions being thrown at me about how my son was doing. It seemed like a shadow of gloom had settled over my head and every time I saw a child walk in, I would stylishly find my way to one of the rest rooms to shed the tears which were clustered in my eyes. When I had spent a few minutes, I would come out, and as cheerily a face as I could muster, I would show the staff around that I was okay and just needed to make use of the toilet. Most of the time, I would mask my pain with childish humour, trying so desperately hard to ensure that no one knew exactly how I felt.

However, for those of our staff members who knew me better, they were able to notice that something was clearly off, as I had changed drastically.

To make matters worse, in our little close-knit community, quite a number of people were aware of Vasili's condition and when they came by my section in the company of their children, they would often attempt to show some empathy. Which whilst was very kind of them it, became more torturous. The more this happened, the less I was able to cope with it and one day, I simply told my brother I couldn't continue on the job because it was simply too mentally strenuous.

I couldn't cope anymore, not with sadness at home and now at work. I had thought work would help lift up my spirits, but I knew too many people around me who wanted to help but were going about it the wrong way. I really didn't want them to bring up Vasili in every conversation, but obviously, a lot of people thought it would help to

talk, to ask me how I was coping with the news of my son's disability and with the reversal of a normal life. This made it even harder to let them know I was only getting more and more shattered by their incessant 'care'. I was simply, done. Strangely enough, although I felt this way, I would bring Vasili up when I needed to express my pain in words or if I wanted to share my experience and to spread awareness of how this happened and when I did, I just couldn't stop the words from pouring out of my mouth. I couldn't win, I didn't want to speak about it but when I wanted to, it had to be on my terms and when I wanted to.

With that, I left the company for my brother to run and continued to live in the exiled gloomy existence that I had been sentenced to. I really did believe it was a life sentence, to live in misery for the rest of one's life was no mere threat, it was my reality.

Since I really couldn't do much work and was almost redundant by now, I employed a solicitor to help me find the answers I so dearly needed answers to.

This was before I sank into depression and had to do a sleeve gastrectomy (the surgery where most of my stomach was removed), and when I got over this, I decided to have a fresh start. Well, that was my plan anyway.

Elena's Diary

So Vasili was declared to be blind on his first few eye tests. We had agreed with our ophthalmologist to not repeat the eye test until a year or so to see if there would be any improvements. There were signs showing us that there had been major improvements, but we needed confirmation from the test. Just a few months later after my dad had passed away I received an appointment letter to repeat his eye test at Birmingham eye clinic.

I went along to the appointment not expecting anything, it was one of many other appointments! I questioned to myself if the eye test would even be successful as the last one was insufficient in my view as he couldn't sit still to even focus on the screens. Nevertheless, we waited patiently for a very long time in the waiting room, having my heart set up ready for the worst!

As we went into the review room we all remembered each other from the last screening, I sat down with Vasili and kept him calm whilst the nurse attached the electrodes to his head. This allows them to measure the response of brainwave patterns, everything was done so quickly and was over within minutes! The doctor went back to the computer to review his results as I sat looking at him through the window. He was silent and seemed shocked to say he couldn't believe it! His exact words were 'he has pretty much normal vision, such a big improvement from the last test results'. I was taken back and needed to hear it a few times, I just couldn't believe it! I walked out the room in shock, I really wasn't expecting anything as positive as that I called my family as soon as I could and shared the news with everyone, also broadcasted the fantastic news on Facebook.

As I began to make my way out of the hospital a white butterfly came towards me. I carried on passed the reception desk and the butterfly followed and landed right on me.

I found it so out of the ordinary to see a butterfly inside the hospital never mind landing on me!! So I searched the internet to see if it resembled anything and it does. White butterflies symbolise past spirits, good luck or angels watching over you. I really felt it was my dad watching over me and that truly topped off the best news ever!

Oblivion to Emotional Intelligence

The human brain is an amazing organ; one that can make a person achieve many great things, but also on the other scale, can totally destroy a person and leave them in despair. I was in the place of being torn apart little by little in utter despair, as was my wife. While seated in a large hospital with the love of my life besides me staring blank in total shock, we were there for each other, yet we both felt so alone.

Having the right positive thoughts are so important to being able to cope with hardships in life and believe me when I say that I was far from ready for this kind of blow to my person, I wasn't ready. I just couldn't take the amount of wreckage that this situation was to unleash on my heart and mind. I mean I literally became ill and disabled by the after effects, and helpless to the extent that the only way I could cope was to bury the realities and fight for answers, to secure the support my family needed, and to help my family.

I was in coping mode. A sense of denial kicked in as I spent many months, even years following this event trying to find the best people to help Vasili but also to spread awareness. I searched the world over for answers and ways to help my King. Writing to the Government for answers and for change, speaking at NHS Patient Safety Leads was a start for change, but it never seemed enough. Even the news of the seven families that were saved from this certain hardship based on the awareness we spread online, via social media and the news coverage was not enough. I NEEDED MORE. I wanted the world to know that my healthy son was made disabled and I could not allow it to happen to others. I quickly realised how small I was and that my message was not as important as that of someone who was, for instance, famous. I was not trendy enough, and neither was the message I wanted to share trendy enough or worthy of the kind of attention I had hoped it would generate, it just wasn't getting the right traction that I wanted it to gain. We had helped a few people but there are many more out there that are yet to hear us and may fall victim of the same ordeal as we did, and I wouldn't want that to happen to anybody.

It's taken me a number of years to get to where I am now, and it continues to be a learning experience. Over time I have come to realise that all these trials that we have faced have actually given us strength and durability. I still feel great pain in my heart as regards to the loss of our planned future for ourselves and that of our children but somehow it has also made us stronger. I named my son My Little Spartan because of his strength, and strangely enough, his hardships have taught us more about ourselves and the Spartan that dwells within us whom we can call upon in trying times. The love of strangers fuels our strength and I feel it is that exact love that has fuelled my son's strength. He feels it from our good carers and from those that show a genuine love towards him, but for those that don't or those that put on a false sense of affection, he also senses it right away and cries.

We noted this with one of our last caregivers who while we were present, would show so much care and love to Vasili, yet on camera we caught her being forceful and non-interactive. My son although trapped by so many difficulties would let us know in his own way that things were not right. It is really amazing just as it is heart-wrenching at the same time knowing that this had gone on for some time. Sometimes, love alone is not enough; faith also has its place but there is a level of emotional intelligence that one has to explore, to be able to find some more meaningful sense of peace.

For me I found this on a property course. YES, as strange as this may sound, it is true. I would regard this course as more of a personal development course than property. In the last year, I have grown up so much and in so many ways. I have attended so many courses as I tried to seek a way forward, hoping to find a way to work from home or to find a more passive work solution that allows me the time with my son and gives me the opportunity of being able to help my wife. In my entrepreneurial quest to find a solution to our monetary but also logistical problems of being self-sufficient with a severely disabled child and an unpredictable existence, I had to find and literally carve a new existence not only for my family but also for myself and for my self- worth. To feel more human, feel like a man again, and to feel competent and useful, to live and not just to exist for the sake of existence.

Although early into my new choice of a career, I had found and met many inspiring and truly humble people; many of whom I had named and shown appreciation to at the prelude of this book. I cannot fully express my appreciation with regards to being associated with positive people that seek to better themselves and the lives of others. It is a value and virtue that truly aligns my heart and aspirations to their own.

My Fresh Start

It is never too late to start afresh and indeed, this is my testimony as regards my work and career in general.

Today, of all the challenges, trials, successes and failures I have encountered in my life, one of my biggest regrets was not being able to have saved my son. But then, I know that we did all we could do; hindsight is indeed a painful place to be when a piece of you is so badly hurt.

Moving forward and as I work out ways to establish some kind of normalcy in my life, I am delighted to state that I am making reasonable career progress. I am into property investing coupled with my digital marketing and design expertise, I am slowly but steadily finding myself again, and it seems pretty interesting to feel myself grow in ways I had never imagined after our terrible ordeal. It takes my mind off all of the stress I have had to pass through in recent times, and it reminds me that indeed, after a lot of pain, it is still very possible to stand strong.

This career choice indeed makes me very grateful to still be alive; and I have found some purpose to my pain, at least a little. Over the years, I have had stints at different careers, done my bit in each, and moved on when I could no longer continue, once I got to realise that it doesn't align with my current situation and unpredictable future. The latest of such is a print design company which I used to run but has become somewhat of a hobby now as I do not have the requisite strength to continue running it as a one-man band. I mean I did it, I created all of the fabulous designs, bought the CNC machines, laser engraving machines, embroidery machines, direct to garment machines and large format printing machines whilst trying - and I say that with great effort -whilst still trying, I was able to achieve a measure of success, but I always wanted to do more, to give more value. Everything is a balancing act and, that for me with lack of sleep and many hospital visits, had truly been a trying period, but it also proved that nothing is impossible! I can continue with the right team, but my effused entrepreneurial soul has found that I function best using my skills away from manning machines and working on my business without being totally enmeshed in the business.

Now, I seem to have found a love for property investing which wouldn't wane and I am so passionate about it. I am also in love with the great personalities and friends I have connected so well with, within the last year of my journey. To some, this is just networking, but to me I have found long and truly strong, meaningful and unwavering friendships that I sincerely value. Something I quickly found after my son was maimed, the valued relationships which I did not have in place before.

Later on, in honour of my son I would like to set up a charity, a kind of foundation for children who have disabilities and to champion their cause. I aspire to achieve a kind of umbrella charity for all disabilities and it is my goal to call it "My Little Spartans". I have to establish my own foundations first and then this will be created, and I hope it will help all those who are in need.

If you search deep enough, there can be purpose in pain and how deep that purpose feels. At least, from my life experience, this is one thing which I have come to understand and accept. I no longer get angry at the environment, the hospital, the government or any other person or organisation which I could blame for my predicament. Instead, I look on with purpose, ready to unravel the course that life has brought my way.

Within the last year, I am proud to say that I have been on a personal development journey, carving out a new 'me', a new 'business'. One that has made me discover that there's only one way to get ahead in life, and that is by finding the Spartan within ourselves; by discovering the hope we truly possess within ourselves and by walking on our own charted paths.

On this journey, I have had to rediscover my person, my passion, my likes and dislikes, as if I were unravelling my personality with a new set of eyes. In this new career path of mine, I have found there to be challenges, but if Vasili could beat all his struggles and all of the other numerous complications along the way and yet smile, how could I, in a good mind, justify giving up? I simply could not. With this as enough inspiration, I have made far more strides than I ever thought I could and right now, I seem to have made significant progress in this career path. I feel as though if I had not gone through so much pain, maybe I wouldn't have been able to navigate through these trying times with such ease. Maybe I would have stayed defeated and never even discovered half of who I am or who I am meant to be. I might have just remained static and been revolving around the same circles. But I can't. With as little as he is, he has changed a lot of things around us, he has improved our attitude towards life and the very people around us. Countless of times he has proved to be a king, despite the impediments that hold him.

With a refreshed grasp of purpose, I now take on challenges routinely, and it is a part of the development of the new 'me' that I wrote about earlier. I look at Vasili and see the amount of pain he's been through and his ability to be gracious through it all. It is quite hard for me to understand how he keeps on going. But for me, I draw out so much inspiration from this living, breathing legend that I have the great privilege of calling my firstborn son. His youth does, in no way, no disrespect to the amount of courage which he has, and that in itself, spurs me on to further develop myself. If he could go through as many surgeries as he's been through, spending as much time under the scrutiny of health care workers and still manage to remain cheerful at all times, then why ought I complain? I would question myself along this line when it seemed as though I was getting quite discouraged.

Indeed, I am eternally grateful to my son, Vasili, for teaching me how to have a new start, and that nothing ever signals the end of you except you allow it to. And as well, I am grateful to my other children for being my sunrise in dark times, and of course, to Elena, the calming force of my life.

Elena Says

Over a year of waiting and seeking medical advice from the NHS services, we finally couldn't wait any longer, we had to pay a private counsellor to help us get through the traumatic event we had experienced. They diagnosed me with PTSD (Post Traumatic Stress Disorder). I had an amazing water birth with my son, it was such a fantastic feeling having a natural birth with barely any pain relief. It was a miracle pregnancy, miracle birth and the fact I never thought I would have a boy it was no wonder I was on cloud nine!!

The water birth resonated every time I had a bath at home and also of the time I was in early stages of labour, I decided to have a bath for pain relief before going into hospital...by the time I got there I was already 5cms dilated.

So every time I had a bath, the scene of the birth would constantly replay and I would physically feel the pains of labour coming back to me, so desperate to go back to that time so I could do everything all over again, this time knowing what I know now about jaundice would of changed the whole series of events. I would wish to put Vasili back in my belly where he was safe and wonder if he had known what was coming, is that the reason why I was ten days overdue? I would cry constantly to what turned out to be an anxious night.

Above all of my other anxieties of doing any normal daily activities, it all seemed to be a struggle. School runs were difficult, going to the park and grieving constantly that my baby couldn't hear his world, the sound of nature. He couldn't see the ducks we went to feed and I would be desperate to go home so I could breakdown into tears and ask myself why I even attempted to go out!! I was trying to carry on, I was trying to relay some of the promises I had made to my daughter Ellie. Although there was one thing they could definitely do together with real joy and that was swimming, the smile on both of their faces was amazing!

I became more comfortable in my own bubble at home until I stepped back out to the real world again and that's when it would hit me back in the face of how much our lives had changed and how different we now were to everyone else.

I felt so upset that I wasn't strong enough to help my husband with his own battles of depression, I couldn't cope with my own feelings never mind trying to deal with others... I would switch off to it all and let him do what he needed to do to grieve in his own way. We both dealt with our feelings so differently. I pretty much shut down whereas Mike wouldn't stop talking about his feelings and what had happened. It was just making me worse to go over things over and over in a vicious circle. I felt a wreck watching him hide away alone, but I fully supported him to do the gastric sleeve in hope it would fix some of his depressing thoughts. But again, I had to be strong, again another surgery, back in hospital with all sorts of worries running through my mind.

Above all this we were always both so strong for each other, on my most weak days he would hold things up for me and vice versa.

I thank my dad for making me strong!

He had been suffering with severe depression for ten years. I and my family had been grieving him whilst he was still alive… we lost the dad we had always known. He would say he felt dead inside and that would make me angry, he could no longer walk unaided and again that would make me angry as I felt he had the ability to walk but chose not to, yet at that same time my son had no ability to and I wished that he had the same choices.

It wasn't until I understood that feeling of being dead inside that I could sympathise with him, maybe I could have also been in the same state of depression but with knowing how it had affected my dad and the impact it had on my whole family, I was determined to seek help and not let myself get to that point. I knew I needed to keep strong as I had no choice. I was a full-time carer for my baby who had just been resuscitated and fought so much for his life that there was no way I was going to give up on him or my family.

I prayed every day for strength to keep us strong, I would pray that Mike would get better as I could see traits of my dad but I was just too weak and didn't know what to do!! Mike also received counselling shortly after being diagnosed with PTSD which really did help us both overcome our initial trauma stage and aided us to live more in the present instead of reliving the past.

Chapter 4:

Elena: A Blend of Beauty and Graciousness |

My Wife did not have it easy in life as well, so I tend to cut her some slack. As a family, I would say that even if we do not know the proper dictionary definitions of pain, we have handled pain, slept for years, and woken up with pain by our bedsides, and slept those same nights with pain almost suffocating us. So, to be sincere, we really have seen a lot.

My wife's father, that is, my father-in-law, was pretty young when he died. He had been considered a true gentleman and I, for one, looked up to him for many years, until eventually, he was diagnosed with a condition that eventually led to his death. Anyway, he had died young and is sorely missed by all.

There is this popular saying that 'you either sink or swim'. It's been hard, but we have been there for each other. Yes, it's been difficult, and we have had our challenges and tribulations, but somehow this rock of beauty has a crystal clear and pure soul, and I am honoured to know and have her as a part of my life. Don't get me wrong, it's taken some serious effort and part of the process was that of detachment to focus on the present.

The detachment process was slow and painful. At first, it was barely noticeable, and I tried convincing myself that it was just as a result of the stress she was definitely going through. But later on, as I began to overeat and started to lose shape, it became apparent that I was indeed, lapsing into another bout of depression. My wife almost completely detached from me, yet somehow this was needed for our growth. Sometimes, you need to fail or reach rock bottom before you either decide to fight for something or someone you so dearly love.

On one hand now, there was Vasili and the terribleness of his state, to cater for and being his mother; she was the one who was in charge of him all the time. On the other hand, her eyes always had the sad burden of a mother that needed help but could not give up the ability to accept all the help she deserved and so desperately needed.

When it was clear that my depression was full blown, as was my obesity, she'd half-heartedly told me to do whatever the doctors wanted me to do because they definitely knew best, right? The effort it took her to bare even that little portion of her heart to me, and I saw how very much that effort was, was one of the few reasons I had agreed to go for the surgery.

Throughout that surgery period, the pre-testing and post evaluation, I had more than a little glimpse of my wife. I saw the love I was once used to seeing in her eyes once more, and I was nudged in the direction of trying again; convinced that any opportunity with her, was worth it. Again, I wish those few moments of our clear display of love would have lasted forever.

50

But as usual, tragedy always seemed to lurk around the corner and was ever ready to strike. That is what I'd come to notice with our life. As usual, Mr. Tragedy just could not allow us to enjoy our newly found intimacy.

One morning, on Vasili's second birthday, my wife received a mail from the doctor's office. They never sent anything by mail, so you can say this was a surprise out of the blue. As we tried to make sense of this singling out experience and started to read out the mail, a new silence settled upon us. We had been cuddling, but slowly, both our bodies became taut, angry almost, at the string of events and what we could possibly have done to deserve such a terrible life.

In that mail was the confirmation for my wife to visit for further tests, in addition to the previous one she had undergone some weeks back. She had been experiencing a severe pain under her ribs to the point where we had to call on the ambulance on a couple of occasions as the pains were so excruciating that she couldn't move lest she trigger it further. Whenever she had to go away like that, the responsibility was mine to stay at home with the kids, after all I could not take my son Vasili along with me, and for my daughter it would often be time to be asleep. Whenever this occurs, once the ambulance staff arrives, she would be rushed into the back of the ambulance where the staff would administer morphine to help soothe her pain. After a stressful period of trying to find someone to cover the home and our kids, I would rush to the hospital after her. The first time it occurred, she was told that the problem could have been severe heart burn. But as the crisis became re-occurring, hospital staff had to conduct several tests and after the series of tests, we were informed that it had nothing to do with heart burn but more in the line of a problem with her liver. Perplexed, my wife asked about what could have caused this and she was given a couple of reasons, one of them was a strong suggestion of cancer. On hearing this, tears freely flowed from both our faces. As the days passed, my wife would lie on the sofa in silence, watching my daughter play whilst sobbing. We could not believe it, we did not have conclusive facts but the idea that it could be cancer- as well as her frantic Google searches didn't aid the situation.

By the time more tests were conducted, and the results obtained, it was with great relief that we confirmed the problem was only with my wife's gall bladder, and for which she had to undergo surgery to get it removed immediately. Thankfully, it was not cancer! I had to hold the fort and be there for my wife during this truly trying period.

However, I am deeply grateful because it could easily have been the original opinion of cancer, but God made it become otherwise, he made it become something that we could better manage and be done with, only within a short time. I truly do not know what I would have done if it had been cancer. I love my wife, and I would never let her suffer alone, I would have been there for her through it all but what would have happened to my children, who would have been there for them? No doubt the strain would have been overwhelming and even more for my daughter, who probably was already smarting from the enormous weight we unconsciously placed on her fragile shoulders, though she carried on with dignity, during the critical period of Vasili's ailment.

During the period of my wife's prognosis, and not too long after it, a dear friend of similar age died from cancer, leaving behind her beloved husband and children. This family had served as another means of inspiration for my family externally, apart from our own son.

As I contemplated the many times things had just refused to turn out well for us even more so, how it seemed that we were jinxed with constant bad luck, I was hurt, angry and can say that I boiled with fury within my person, for the many times it felt as though there was no hope. Anything else? I would question and challenge the world, shouting in my car as I sat in a quiet field near our home. My wife was completely oblivious to this habit of mine. For at least 3 weeks before this point, my own mind was a jumble and before we had confirmation that the suspected cancer was indeed only something quite minor and her symptoms were as a result of her gall bladder bile leaking into her liver and mimicking the heightened liver enzymes results.

When I heard that there was a NO cancer verdict, I was ecstatic! We were both obviously in immense relief, almost on a high. The scare was all we needed to remind us of what we had or have, and that we did not lose it all, as our minds had already tricked us into believing what was not. It allowed us a deeper appreciation for what we had and how much we so cherish it dearly, and it also brought us to the realisation of how long we had taken it for granted. True! It may have seemed so, and this is not to make light the challenge we came to encounter every day, but it opened our hearts and minds to the appreciation of what we still had, the joy that should exist in our lives and how we shouldn't take that for granted, ever. On hearing the news and on realisation of the immense joy it brought to my soul, it became more apparent that I had to let go of my selfish thoughts of 'why me?' and to rather focus on my life as it was, not how I wanted it to be.

Before this day of relief though, I was living in the hope that it was not cancer. I remember that I drove home ready to be a man and to handle what we had been dealt with, just like my son had to. I rushed to my wife who had just put the kids to sleep, I could see she was not herself, and for the first time in a long time I could see her saddened soul. I tried to help my wife by resuming our long overdue cuddling.

We postponed regular schedules, still revelling in the new love we had found and holding tightly to each other like we could predict that something wrong was going to happen again. We loved each other and that was enough.

The first time I drove her to the doctors on the cusp of finding out the truth, all I could do throughout that drive was to think deeply, as my heart was in my mouth and I was intensely over thinking everything, questioning - What if she really did have cancer? What if she died from it? What would happen to the kids? What would happen to me?

I glanced furtively at her every once in a while, but she was obviously too lost in her thoughts to humour me with corresponding looks or even an acknowledgement of my stares. She was beautiful, this woman seated beside me, so beautiful.

I whispered, 'You are beautiful.'

She smiled and placed a hand on my shoulder as if to say, 'Don't worry; you don't have to say things you don't mean just to make me feel good.' But I did mean it, every word of it, and if this would be the last time I could say it before our world would once again be overturned, I was going to say it with the deepest conviction I had.

So, I slowed down the car to a halt about 15 minutes before we would have reached the hospital and said, once again: 'YOU are beautiful. I love you so much, and I always will, regardless of what... what we are told today. You are my wife; you always will be the love of my life!'

I saw her eyes shimmer; she was on the brink of tears. We had no idea how this day would go but at least, she was certain of my undying love for her and that alone, was quite the comfort she needed in such a time as this.

I continued 'You know I would write it down for you and create something beautiful, but well, you married this dyslexic guy that writes poems'. She laughed; she knows I have an issue with dyslexia, but it has never stopped me from trying and she has known me as a little bit of a poet, and we openly joke about the grammar mistakes in poems I had previously written for her. No; it reminded me, as effectively as it possibly could, of our relationship before and how much effort we both applied to our courtship.

My wife was so happy; it almost burst forth through her. In that 15 minutes' drive, I saw her exhibit a fraction of the joy I'd seen shining in her eyes in those months immediately before Vasili was born. I wished that I could hold on to those moments forever, seeing as I didn't even know what the result of her tests would be at that time.

It became clear to me that Vasili is a blessing to the family. Our son, that God has sent to us to change our perspective in Life, making us appreciate the absurdly beautiful things in life that we ordinarily wouldn't have taken a second look at. It has helped us to expect the worst, not that we are people with a negative mind, but we have been trained and built up over time to handle whatever comes our way.

Thankfully, all was okay as I explained earlier. But it does show how no matter the challenges and sorrows we all find in our paths on our journey in life, there is always something else. We must all give in, accept and make good of what we can lay hold of. No matter the challenges we have faced.

My wife became pregnant again barely a year after my son. We had somewhat planned it because we felt my daughter needed the sibling she so wished for and that would not take away from Vasili but we wanted to have a bigger family and so we just pushed things forward a little to aid her. After all, we knew as Vasili grew older that it would be more of a challenge looking after him and handling him whilst handling a needy baby alongside would only be making it harder on ourselves. We felt we needed to do this at this time even though we were not really ready for another baby. But we did not want to lose our dreams and aspirations as a family and no one or any challenge was going to rob us of that.

I digressed then onto my children whilst I was expressing my thoughts about my beautiful wife and yet they are all interlinked. The strength they have within them is a testament to my wife's super power, the same super power that made me fall in love with her when I was not even thinking of settling down.

For some amazing and humbling reason, she chose me and for this, regardless of all our difficulties, I would not change a thing; I would go through the pains and hardships to meet this special lady over and over again.

In life, it is rare to find such a beauty and I am blessed by all four of my beauties. They are what I call my four pillars; my pillars of strength. Like in typical ancestral Greek, myths are born from true stories that are slightly exaggerated. I wish this story was exaggerated but its real life, our real life. Myths become legends but in real life I exist alongside legends that inspire me to be a strong and a better person. We all have them around us in many forms. What is your inspiration that keeps you strong? We all have one if only it is the need to live. It is the gift of life we must appreciate and the loss of life we must appreciate even more. The maimed by disability are here for constant reminders; maybe just maybe I needed that constant reminder and if I personally did not, someone will be looking at our family and will be reminded about how fortunate they are.

In all, through all of these extremely trying times, Elena has been a blend of beauty and graciousness, never allowing herself to be so absorbed in self-pity and sorrow for too long. Even now, with my newly found passion for life and the new course which I'm choosing to take, it is only through her love and support that I've been able to come this far. Without her, I'm pretty confident that I wouldn't have been able to make it through to the other side.

When I think about my life and the blessings which I've been granted, I count Elena over and over again. Truthfully, I am amazed at how much strength she possesses, how much she can firmly mix love and calmness, patience and strength, determination and loving tenderness. Probably, my marriage to her is why I am still alive, and it definitely is why I'm able to encourage others.

SECTION II:
ON DISABILITY-JOYS AND PAINS

Chapter 5:

Vasili's Story: The Journey |

I feel like I have aged ten years above my real age since my little Spartan was born. One sure thing, however, is that I have gained so much resilience. I have learnt from Vasili how fighting one more round makes you capable of fighting the next round. How one can go from one challenge to another, and still come out victorious. Indeed, this is what Vasili has taught me, and he has done so by simply having me look at him fight once more, and then once more, and then once again.

Vasili Kalisperas, our little Spartan, was born on the 18th of May 2012. When he was born, he was absolutely healthy. The kind of child you saw and fell instantly in love with for his handsomeness and perceived strength. He had been born overdue, and was allowed to come home the same day, in all his glory.

Vasili's birth filled me with a certain wave of pride; one so strong, I couldn't dare deny. I was a very proud father. This was not just because he was a boy, although that certainly made me glow some; (as statistics claim most fathers want at least one boy) but of a truth, I love my daughters equally. There is something special about continuing the family name and having an equal balance of kids to satisfy your duties as a procreator. For me, one of the most satisfying things I was able to do, was to pass on the tradition of naming him after the most inspirational man in my life, my father; a man who, in my eyes, can simply do no wrong and who is strong, inspiring, wise, calm, supportive and selfless.

As men, we have a place in the world that normally consists of taking the trash out, putting up Christmas lights, carrying the heaviest child on shopping trips - all the usual manly stereotypical duties. And boy, there are many.

But, as this tragedy gradually unfolded, I realised early on, that these duties are also carried out, and beautifully too, by Elena when I'm not around. I also realised that I had to help more and take a fair enough share of the burden off of her. I have, in essence, embraced my feminine side, a side I never knew I had. It was a decision I chose to make, to ensure she still had a glow in her beautiful eyes (I wrote a poem for her at the end of this book) and yes, I can hear all of my friends laughing right now.

Truly, I have my dad to thank for this, he is my inspiration and I'm proud to say he has always helped my mum from day one and they have always had the most amazing strong marriage that anyone would be envious of, and which I had always aimed towards, and loved to emulate.

Vasili's birth was the best thing in our lives, we were all so proud. My wife was happy that the birth had progressed so smoothly, with no complications. As with all pregnancies, fear, love, hope, stress and pain all play a part of your emotions. Emotions that I like to call 'life feelings'.

I know that God didn't promise us a smooth journey in life, but somehow when you're in a bubble, you expect it. I drive nice cars, I have a lovely house and my family seemed perfect, so why would I expect sadness to come knocking? After all, for my entire life, I had believed in God (although I didn't really practice or focus enough on him). I knew doing good and not bad was the right way to live, but that was about all.

Something was coming to shatter all this. The speed at which it hit us was mind blowing. Not just because of the enormity of the situation, but also because the deadly tentacles of the problem was spreading out far and wide, and almost seemed endless in its extensions. It seemed like it was wrapped in so many papers and like an onion, the more layers we peeled off meant we had many more layers to peel off. Indeed, the stress we felt was immense and seemingly endless.

My son Vasili was born healthy and fine and we were discharged the same day; he fed well and seemed focused on us, being playful and very alert.

However, within only one day, he began to appear severely jaundiced (yellowing on his face first). The first midwife was due to visit so we thought we would ask her opinion. When she arrived, she seemed lovely and spoke to my wife for a brief period. The colour of his skin did not seem to faze her, and she reassured both my troubled wife and the whole family (who had come to congratulate us on Vasili's birth), that this was common in new babies.

The reassurance was definite and unwavering, so we relaxed after all, our first daughter had also been jaundiced after she was born (although hers was not until a few weeks later). A day later, Vasili became less enthusiastic on feeding and he seemed more tired. We rang the emergency midwife. Within the hour, she came and noted his orange appearance and called in for a review. We immediately took Vasili to hospital, but we thought it would just be for a check- up.

After waiting a while, they took Vasili for observation under special hospital lights. At this point, no one seemed interested in talking to us, we weren't as much as told what measures they were taking and why they were taking such measures, all we could do was sit outside the glass walled room, looking in.

We watched, as the doctors placed my son under the blue lights. Suddenly I saw my son's body flop and the emergent re- sponse of the emergency staff, which all began to act out in disordered synchrony, evidence of their frantic confusion. We were quickly ushered into another room, away from the scene. At this point, our world began to collapse, slowly but surely.

We were in the baby unit, so we kept on waiting for a baby cry to see if it was Vasili. We heard several, so we could not be sure if it was our boy or if we had simply lost him. I couldn't bear the thought of losing him, but with everything that was happening so fast like in a movie, I really thought he was gone.

Elena remained in a state of shock, but her patience seemed totally unwavering. It was with this strong patience that she waited for us to take him home and carry on with our lives. I will never forget how calm she was, that tragic day.

I knew she was no longer herself, and from this point, deep in my heart, somehow I knew what was to come. To say the least, we had lapsed into a state of denial. I knew from the nurses' faces as they passed by us, that something major had happened to Vasili. I am usually able to read through the thin line shielding real expressions from apparently showing on people's faces and this ability still remained; my instincts not fading in the least, even in my terribly shocked state.

Yet, I wished myself wrong, at least this one time. I kept wishing I was wrong, so I desperately tried to hold on to hope.

Some hours went by, and eventually a nurse came to speak to us saying he was now stable. I asked all the questions, questions my heart did not want to ask but to which my brain was demanding answers. Vasili later underwent a blood transfusion which took several hours, and because of which we spent the night in hospital.

It was then that a new sense of realisation began to dawn on me, that my son – as he had been for those first few precious days – was lost after the second day in intensive care. Yes, he was now 'stable', but it really looked like he was gone. We saw the twisting of his neck and arching of his back and were told that these were all signs of Kernicterus.

Every single day, we stayed in hospital by his bedside. We did this for nearly a month; trying to balance spending the needed time with him at the hospital, against a normal life for our four-year-old lively daughter, while, in the process, trying to shield and protect her from the pain and anguish we were drowning in. It was hard, very hard, for me to handle all of this. Watching his family deteriorate is the hardest thing any man could imagine! The feeling of failure would also stab at your heart. I felt as though I had failed them. I felt that maybe I could have done something to prevent all of this, something, whatever it was. It was my responsibility to keep them safe, to be the man, and yet somehow, they are disintegrating right under my nose and I seem very helpless to stop it, to do anything, to change the course of events. The trauma is crippling.

During this baffling period, I'd once stood at the side of his incubator box with all the lights and wires; the look on his face was such a sad one. I could have sworn that his eyes had sadness in them, and in addition, it had a plea for help. This broke me, and the next thing was that I began to cry. This was particularly important because then, it became obvious to me, that this was the most terrible situation that had ever befallen me as an individual, for I never usually cry, I find it too hard; and even at my best friend's funeral I didn't shed a single tear, let alone my grandfather's funeral years a few years earlier.

Usually, I am able to rein my feelings in, and even help in comforting others; but watching his eyes filled with fear and that plea for help completely broke me. He was helpless, and so was I. Completely helpless, and the worst feeling for a parent was helplessness; not being able to help his/her child out of a certain predicament. I don't think anything could break a parent's heart more.

Once I started crying, my wife immediately followed suit, crying more than she had in days earlier. She had never seen me cry, and it broke her heart too, to see her man of several years break down and weep like a baby. I noticed the nursing staff had started to cry too, which took me by surprise. Sensing that everyone was losing their composure and calm because of me, I started to compose myself for my family and ironically, for the staff at the hospital too.

The first couple of weeks which we spent at the hospital felt like years to us, so much happened, that I could actually write a book on his first two weeks of stay in the hospital, and indeed, I wish I could, but my life is too hectic and busy for me to do that. Our diary seems to dictate our lives now, it is a small Art Deco book my wife keeps to arrange everything we do.

Although I've currently begun to work again (read my work story in another chapter), and I find some sense of escapism there, my trauma still haunts me and any opportunity I find to speak to a customer about what has happened to Vasili, I grab. I often find out later, that I made them uncomfortable because they didn't know how to react, especially because the story is so devastating that most people can't comprehend how one can actually bring a healthy baby home, only for his health to be reversed by sheer negligence. But then, it's been good and therapeutic telling people about it, not because I need their pity or sympathy, (in fact I do hate that), but just so that they are encouraged. And it has had that effect many times. They are not only encouraged to hold their heads high when faced with challenges, even if different from ours, they become informed for when it is their turn to give birth.

I've had someone ask me before if Vasili was our first child. She was surprised that it would happen to us even when it was not our first time of childbirth. When I told her that he had an older sister, she could not hide her shock. Initially, she had concluded that we didn't know what to do because we had not had a baby before then, but when she learnt about Ellie, she was able to put together some thoughts. She said that it must have been because Vasili was our second child and was deemed low risk because of a healthy pregnancy.

This was actually a very wrong notion, as every child is special and thus requires all the love, information, and treatment plus care possible.

Her words struck me, and even though I have been trying to get health institutions to do the right thing, I am on my own, prepared to take some of the responsibilities. So, once an opportunity presents itself, I take it. I tell them about preventative measures, signs, and how to deal with Kernicterus. I also tell them about how strong our son has been all through this, even though he is just a little boy. I tell pregnant ladies to be very mindful, and not of hospitals this time around, after all it was a renowned hospital that helped to deliver Vasili. I advise them to ask questions and ensure that tests are conducted. I tell them to insist on check-ups, after ensuring that possible pre-natal causes are taken out of the way. I let them know that any strange colour or behaviour exhibited on their baby should be attended to because you never can say. It might not be jaundice, it could even be a deadlier disease. Well, a lot of them I have met since, are doing very well today.

Meanwhile, I really think I should share with you, one parent that turned up to give an unexpected testimony. Their child developed Cerebral Palsy. All I told the father was to adopt the measures that I had shared with him earlier on, and he accepted that information which at times, if not preventative, are either curative or adaptive. Especially since some things just find their way to spring up. Even after so much grooming which ought to get them scrapped and impossible to sprout, has been done. The girl now walks and is actually doing fine in her schooling.

68

Really, a lot of people have learnt from Vasili, either directly or indirectly, and I am very happy and proud of that. I am one of the very few persons that believe that even if you don't get to achieve something, you should teach others how to achieve it. Many think that it certifies their loss, but the truth is that the blessing and satisfaction that comes from someone gaining from your wealth of knowledge or river of experience is awesome. I have my pains still, but that's enough.

My heart has been chipped away; nothing hurts me more than to see my poor wife silently cry when she thinks everybody is fast asleep. Her strength is amazing, yet I know she's not immune to a breakdown. Her life has been hard. The last few years has brought much sadness to us all.

My wife's father became depressed and was diagnosed as suffering from mental illness. Also, my brother-in-law and uncle were diagnosed with cancer, but what happened to our son takes first place for pain. Nothing, absolutely nothing, can explain the anguish we feel. I do feel though, that God was preparing us for the immense pain we were about to become encapsulated by. Without these traumas, we would have probably felt the pain even harder.

My life is a balance between getting justice and helping my family on a day to day basis. Through the hospital's own internal investigations, we later found out the midwife that visited us that fateful afternoon was a student unaccompanied by her mentor. We also found out she had made a previous mistake with another child; although, thankfully, I was reassured that this child's health was not affected.

In one drastic moment, our lives had now changed and my renewed purpose for living was to love and support my family as best as I could. But even this was challenging, with all the torment within me. I researched all that midwives had to learn in regards to the condition my son became victim to, and be examined on it to become qualified. Kernicterus has such a debilitating effect, yet it is highly preventable.

And so, midwives are trained in taking immediate actions or should at least take a Bilirubin meter to check the level of toxicity in the blood.

We were told to put him in the light, something we found many midwives wrongly prescribed to other children suffering this fate. The midwifery guidelines actually state that immediate actions should be taken as this could cause Kernicterus brain damage, damage to certain areas of the brain especially to the part of the brain that is called the basal ganglia and damage can occur especially within 24 hours of birth.

I reached out to certain organisations, such as PICK - Parents of Infants and Children with Kernicterus. Indeed, I must say that all of the members have been amazing and have touched our hearts tremendously. We have actually touched each other's lives.

Elena's Diary

When he turned one year of age we had to make one of the biggest decisions we have ever made, and that was to take the risk in a cochlear implant. This is to give him some sound back after several hearing tests had confirmed that Vasili was profoundly deaf. There was a very scary chance that the cochlear implant would not be successful and undergoing a five-hour operation under sedation was such a scary thought! We felt so vulnerable but with faith in God and trust in the amazing surgeons and cochlear implant team, we decided to go ahead. The glimmer of hope that my baby may hear my voice once again was so heart-warming. I was praying for a miracle as the surgeon didn't want to get our hopes up too much.

Without going into details, thankfully it was the best decision we had made! It had opened up Vasilis world to sound again, and although robotic, he didn't know any other way. And he was showing pleasure from all kinds of sounds!!

We attended an appointment at the cochlear implant team where the hearing processor was switched on for the first time and there were smiles all around. What a relief, we were so happy that we were able to give something back!

On our way home I almost couldn't believe that he could hear me!! I just couldn't stop saying sorry! I wept and apologised and said I was so sorry for letting him down!! I called my family to share the great news and we all cried happy tears.

The first thing I did when we got home was show him all his toys that he never knew made any noise. He smiled and we talked nonstop. Life had definitely changed for us now. He wouldn't get so startled because he knew if I was walking towards him. I could give him cues, I could comfort him with lullabies, and he could hear the music that we would always dance to. Life was better for him.

Because of this success, we then went on to do the second cochlear implant when he was two years old which was also a successful procedure. We are very thankful for these two very special blessings.

Until this day I just cannot believe the strength in my baby and this makes me so proud. He has endured so much pain it's unbearable, but his beautiful angelic soul has shone through in patience and calmness. He always smiles and is such a loving child. We are so happy he fought for his life. It's the most traumatic event we have ever experienced, and I wouldn't wish it on anybody. No mother deserves to have a healthy child taken away from them. No child deserves to have their independence and future taken away from them.

Our priest, Father Christo, has also been of great support and encouragement throughout our troubled times, as have his daughter and son-in-law who themselves witnessed their own pain of disability and loss recently. Our hearts are always with you Ioanna; you will forever be entwined in our thoughts and prayers.

Like so many children impaled with Kernicterus, Vasili is still a beautiful boy with a huge personality. He is now 5 years old and since he was about 6 months old, we have been undergoing counselling as a family. Although we take tablets to deal with depression, nothing can numb or curb our love and support for our family.

The weeks and months which followed his birth were full of constant meetings, scans, tests and therapy work. Our spare time, since then, if we had any, was sacrificed for a new love and a new cause. The trauma was indeed a nightmare, as the healthy birth of our son was reversed so quickly and the memory of what we all had been through continued to haunt us on a daily basis.

To watch a small baby's body go through an MRI machine was indeed a hard scenario for the both of us. To see his little feet sticking out ultimately broke my heart. It was, and still is, the same with EEG scans; although he has definitely grown bigger and seemingly stronger. No child or parent should go through this, to see their perfect baby destroyed by Kernicterus and poor training.

To hear that Vasili is blind, that he can't hear or see and that he has severe Cerebral Palsy, plus other interlinked issues, is just the beginning.

Whilst in intensive care Vasili was fed via an NG tube through his nostrils. We noticed that he could suck our little finger, and so Elena tried to breast feed him again he latched on but we decided it would be best to express and give via bottle for when Elena had to be away with her daughter. For the first few months, he could only manage a small amount of milk and would take hours to feed, by which time he was due for his next feed. Because of this, my wife and I struggled to sleep for more than a couple of hours a night and we were mostly exhausted.

We were advised to go back to feeding via a tube, but because we knew Vasili had some ability to suckle, we wanted him to at least have something a bit 'normal' in his life, so we carried on.

Our perseverance paid off, and eventually Vasili learnt how to drink his milk as a normal child would - well almost normally, as Cerebral Palsy is known to contract muscles including the vocal muscles causing the odd moment to choke, which we had to consistently keep an eye on. However, we are very thankful for his accomplishments.

My children make me immensely proud. The grace with which they all are dealing with the situation has inspired me to try to do more with them. Sadly, Vasili has lost the majority of his primary senses, and it makes it harder for him to accomplish much more. But, we endeavour to try our best, as he is our Little Spartan and he fought for us, as we will for him. Initially, my daughter also struggled to understand why he could not see, hear or walk; but as she becomes older, she has also increasingly become compassionate plain enough to be seen.

I know in my heart, that there is so much pain to come. Yet denial can be a place of comfort, at least in the short term. Vasili's problems have indeed increased, and the level of his disability, as the sheer magnitude of what has happened to him unwinds itself. This has taken some years to reveal, but it is already blatantly, painfully clear, the problems that await us.

The negligence inflicted on him cannot and would not take away our love for him. I know he feels our every touch especially my wife's as well as her beautiful heart and soul full of love and goodness that somehow flows through to Vasili.

He knows our love, he finds peace in our love and we find peace in his, even through his cries of pain. We can only comfort him, let him know he's safe and that we will do all we can for him because he is our saviour. Yes, that's right. Strangely, his pain has saved our souls and taught us all the merits of family love and the real purpose of life.

Through all the pain and anguish, the truth is this: I know my son is our Angel. He is going through all of this pain to teach us all a lesson - a lesson not to take life for granted but to do all you can to prolong it and enjoy what you can. He has lost so much, as have we. Yet we have gained something more. We have gained faith, a belief that there is a reason to stay on. Maybe we are desperate and need something to cling to. I have seen sights I would never have believed possible. I have been touched by my son's grace. I cannot deny him. This is my strength.

A lot of people that see me today, read my notes and listen to me, cannot stop wondering why my wife and I look so fine even with all that we have been through. They expect to see us hide the Spartan that tries to reveal himself in Vasili, somewhere at the corner of the house. They have asked, and my answer will always be that Kernicterus is no sign of weakness. We are strong in spite of the many challenges that do constantly stare us in the faces. This is not a storm that you know goes away after a while, it has come to stay. But like I said earlier, I don't feel the pain as much as I used to. I know that as time goes on, we will be strengthened so much that this is no longer something that we remember to talk about, Vasili included.

We have learnt to deal with it and have come out strong because really, what makes people remain down is their attachment to that which has made them fall. They keep looking back, asking questions, sometimes blaming God, wishing that things were different without forging ahead to find a solution, or embrace the most enjoyable part of the pain, where it cannot be removed.

You see, my strength is held not only by my belief, but also through what I have witnessed. I've seen the light - I know the rocky road ahead and I'm not taking a plane. We will confront this the right way as a family.

It's true, what they say; that love is all you need.

Chapter 6:

Vasili's Ordeal with Kernicterus and Cerebral Palsy |

Still in the spirit of educating as I inform, I have thought it wise to let you in on what Kernicterus and Cerebral Palsy is all about. Like I said earlier, I have had to research to become familiar with my son's condition not only to help me better accept it, but to also be informed on the best ways to deal with it and give care.

Kernicterus actually means 'yellow kern' and the term was used as early as the 1800s. It refers to a brain pathology caused by an accumulation of a substance known as bilirubin within certain brain areas- basal ganglia and a few other areas which are literally stained with bilirubin and begin to look yellow.

Bilirubin is a product of metabolism which, when produced in higher than normal amounts, causes yellowness of the eyes and in newborns, can progress to cause bilirubin-induced neuronal damage (BIND). That is, certain elements of the nervous system are affected grossly by high amounts of bilirubin in the bloodstream. Normally, when there are high amounts of this neurotoxic substance within the bloodstream, what happens in adults is that it rarely gets into the brain because of a protective barrier known as the blood-brain barrier. But in children, newborns especially, this barrier is not yet fully formed. And so, bilirubin crosses into the brain without much hindrance - and you know what happens next.

KERNICTERUS - this is a very rare type of brain damage that occurs in a newborn with severe jaundice. It happens when the metabolite bilirubin in the blood builds up to very high levels and spreads into the brain tissue causing permanent brain damage. But note this; it can be prevented if the causative condition, which is jaundice, is detected and treated early enough before it causes any damage.

What Causes Kernicterus?

Kernicterus is caused by a high level of bilirubin in a baby's blood. If it's left untreated, the bilirubin can then spread into the brain where it causes long-term damage. A low-level build-up of bilirubin is normal. Like I have said earlier, and you would also find out if you make some research or speak with a health care practitioner.

When a child has a low level of bilirubin, it can be referred to as mild jaundice, and this gives the newborn a slightly yellowish tint to the skin and sometimes the eyes. Every newborn has bilirubin in his or her bloodstream and this is normally removed from the bloodstream by the liver and kidneys. Bilirubin leaves the body in urine and stool. During pregnancy, the mother's body removes the extra bilirubin for the baby. After birth, it takes a few days for the newborn's liver to get good at removing bilirubin from the blood. If the baby is fed regularly, say every 2 to 3 hours, mild jaundice will usually go away on its own after a few days. But please note this; if your baby has any signs of jaundice, make sure your doctor is made aware and the child be closely monitored.

This is because if jaundice continues to get worse and is not treated, bilirubin in the blood can build up to a high level and it is at this point that kernicterus becomes a concern. There are quite a number of reasons why some babies would have much higher bilirubin levels than some others. It might be that those babies have health problems that make them more likely to have bilirubin levels that climb to high levels, or in some other situations where the mother's Rh blood factor is incompatible with that of her baby's. Intestinal blockages have been said to also make it harder for a baby to remove bilirubin.

What Are the Symptoms?

Kernicterus is likely to have already started if a baby has certain symptoms, which include:

- Extreme sleepiness and lethargy: This is where a baby sleeps for too long, is quite difficult to wake up from sleep, or can't be kept awake. But be mindful that new-born babies sleep a lot. Lethargy in a newborn can easily be confused with normal newborn behaviour. A lethargic baby does not eat well, does not respond to touching or does not startle from sudden movements, and never seems to fully wake up.

- A very high-pitched cry that does not sound normal.

- Poor muscle tone: The baby may seem "floppy" and weak. Sometimes this is followed by periods when the baby's muscles flex in a way that is not normal.

- The baby may be stiff and arch his or her back and head.
- A fever that occurs along with any of these other symptoms.

The lifelong damage from Kernicterus may cause long- term:

- Movement problems: A baby may develop slow and uncontrolled movements or random jerky movements.
- Hearing loss or deafness: Some babies may seem to have normal hearing, but can also develop a problem, processing sounds.
- Learning problems and other developmental disabilities.
- Problems moving the eyes, especially looking upward.

How Is Kernicterus Diagnosed?

If you believe your child is at risk, it is best to take that child to the hospital immediately. It is important that you have a doctor examine the child and arrive at a valid prognosis on what may be the problem. Please do not resort to self-help or wishful thinking, a little effort on your part could avert a nasty situation. For diagnosis of Kernicterus, your doctor would conduct physical examinations and would possibly recommend some blood tests to determine the bilirubin levels and if containable, would order phototherapy treatments and any other treatment deemed fit. I am not a doctor, I am only sharing my own experience and knowledge that I have had to acquire to help me better understand the condition, accept and seek ways to better manage it.

Once a baby has been diagnosed with Kernicterus, brain damage has already occurred. For this reason, it is very important to follow through and treat jaundice before bilirubin levels get too high.

Can Kernicterus Be Prevented?

Yes it can! But it would require your vigilance and a lot more of your knowledge of the symptoms of jaundice, and your ability to make sure your baby gets testing and treatment immediately.

If your baby is still at the hospital and has signs of jaundice, your doctor or nurse may conduct a bilirubin test. It is absolutely fine to request it. A blood test can check your baby's bilirubin level. A baby with a bilirubin level that requires treatment will have light therapy (phototherapy). This is usually given in the hospital. In very mild cases, you may treat your baby at home using the lights the doctor gives you. Do not be alarmed if your baby has to have phototherapy; it does not mean that he or she is in danger of having brain damage. The doctors use this therapy to help prevent bilirubin from getting to a dangerous level.

Try as much to ensure your baby is fed at least every 2 to 3 hours during the first week or two. This will help keep bilirubin moving out of the body through urine and stool.

It is okay to have your baby thoroughly checked up before you leave the hospital, do not be in a hurry to leave for home. Jaundice is usually at its worst around day 5, so have the doctor or midwife visit within the first 5 days after your child's birth, and when they can't visit, please take the child to the hospital for checks, it's better safe than sorry. Inform the doctor or midwife of any change in colour or yellowing of the skin or eyes. Get medical help right away if you think your baby is jaundiced and is hard to wake, acts very fussy, or is not feeding well.

You can share your concerns with your doctor and find out what may or may not be likely causes for your baby getting Kernicterus. Some of the likely causes include:

- Being born early (more than 2 weeks before the due date).
- Having jaundice in the first 24 hours after birth.
- Having problems with breastfeeding.
- Having bruises or bleeding on the head from a difficult birth.
- Having an older brother or sister who received light therapy for jaundice.

How is it treated?

Quick treatment may help to prevent further brain damage. Treatment may start with light therapy and fluids given through a needle into a vein (intravenous fluid replacement). Sometimes a baby may also have a tube placed down his or her throat or into the stomach for feeding with a special type of formula. Then is most likely to have a blood type test to help determine his or her blood and get them prepared for blood transfusion should the need arise. A blood transfusion may be given to help remove extra bilirubin from the baby's blood.

Long-term treatment for brain damage will depend on a child's specific problems. Typical treatment includes physical therapy, speech therapy, and special education.

Cerebral Palsy

Cerebral palsy, or CP, as it is sometimes called, is a group of disorders that affects balance, movement, and muscle tone. "Cerebral" means that the disorder is associated with the brain, and "palsy" referring to weakness or a muscle problem.

CP starts in the area of the brain that controls the child's ability to move his or her muscles. Cerebral Palsy can happen when that part of the brain doesn't develop as it should, or when it is damaged at about the time of birth or very early on in the life of the child. Not all children were born with CP. Some are referred to as acquired CP and this is when the child develops CP right after birth as is the case with my little Spartan Vasili. Those born with the condition, are said to suffer from congenital CP.

Most sufferers from Cerebral Palsy would have mild or severe issues with muscle control, in some it is so severe that they won't be able to walk on their own. Some people with CP have difficulty speaking and others may have intellectual disabilities, while many have normal intelligence.

What Can Cause it?

Doctors are not always certain about what exactly may be responsible for such damage to the brain or what would have

83

disrupted its development, causing CP, but some of the problems that can damage the brain or disrupt its growth can include:

- Bleeding in the brain while the baby is in the womb, during birth or afterward
- A lack of blood flow to important organs
- Seizures at birth or in the first month of life
- Some genetic conditions
- Traumatic brain injuries

Am I at Risk of Having a Child With CP?

The truth remains that it could happen to anyone, there are no guarantees. But unlike Vasili's whose primary cause was negligence, there are a few conditions while you're pregnant that can increase the chances of your baby developing CP. This is not to say that all of these conditions are definite indicators to having a child who will develop CP, but it is only to enlighten on some of the medically proven situations that are most likely to trigger having a child develop congenital CP. Some of the situations include:

- Being pregnant with multiples, such as twins or triplets
- Having a health issue such as seizures or a problem with your thyroid gland
- Having blood that's not compatible with your baby's, which is also called Rh disease
- Coming in contact with a toxic substance such as mercury which is found in some kinds of fish

You also stand a grave chance of your loved one developing congenital CP if you happen to contract certain infections and viruses during pregnancy. These can also increase the risk of your baby being born with Cerebral Palsy. Some of the bacteria and viruses include:

- Rubella, or German measles, a viral illness that can be prevented with a vaccine
- Chickenpox, also called Varicella (a vaccine can prevent this contagious illness.)
- Cytomegalovirus, which causes flulike symptoms in the mother
- Herpes, which can be passed from mother to unborn child and can damage the baby's developing nervous system
- Toxoplasmosis, which is carried by parasites found in soil, cat faeces and tainted food
- Syphilis, a sexually transmitted bacterial infection
- Zika, a virus carried by mosquitoes

Can My Baby Have CP Even If I Don't Have any High-Risk Conditions?

So much as illnesses in the mother can raise the chances of the child developing CP, so also are some infections in babies liable to causing the development of CP. Here are a few of them:

- Severe jaundice (yellowing of the skin): This condition occurs when excessive bilirubin accumulates in the blood.

- Bacterial meningitis: It causes swelling in the brain and tissues around the spinal cord.
- Viral encephalitis: This also can cause swelling around the brain and spinal cord.

There are also certain other problems that occur during childbirth which can also increase the risk of developing Cerebral Palsy. These include:

- Breech position: This is when the baby is settled in feet-first rather than headfirst when labour begins.
- Low birth weight: If your baby weighs less than 5.5 pounds, the chances for developing CP go up.
- Premature birth: This refers to any birth delivery that occurs anytime under 37 weeks into the pregnancy.
- Complicated labour and delivery: It could mean problems with your baby's breathing or circulatory system as a result of a difficult birth or prolong labour.

I have gone this extra mile to make intending parents become more aware of the condition, being that knowledge is power, and to also give information that we were not made aware of in the early days of Vasili's treatment. Like I have said, this situation was avoidable if only I knew this much or the midwife who came to the house had known enough to look closely at him or so many other "if not's" and "if only's". But as a family, we have chosen not to dwell on them but to channel our energy into making a better life for Vasili and his sisters. It may be daunting at first but as we go along, we find strength in our shared experience and in the daily lessons he teaches us.

As we have seen from the above, Bilirubin encephalopathy, also known as Kernicterus, has a number of several long-term effects, some of which we have seen in Vasili, including hearing loss, seizures and loss of sight. It feels deeply unsatisfying to watch my son being unable to hear the sounds in his environment. And in combination with a loss of sight, it becomes almost impossible to communicate with him. But he finds a way to communicate with us, by speaking, by identifying our touch with smiles and by doing all of the little things which make him so dear to us.

However, it can very easily be prevented and that is sort of ironic; but in our health care delivery system, some things seem to be placed above others. For instance, Kernicterus is a 'never' event in the United States because a routine bilirubin screening is done for kids before they are discharged from the hospital, and this helps to pick out those kids who are at risk of developing severe Neonatal Jaundice, Bilirubin Encephalopathy and Kernicterus. However, in our system in England, it is felt by those at the top of the health care ladder that if this is done, it would prolong the child's hospital stay and that it could also disturb breast-feeding. Such flimsy excuses, as regards the prevention of a condition so severe, it can result in lifetime morbidity- as in Vasili's case, it has.

Sometimes I wonder if they think that we aren't humans. We, the ones who have to suffer from their lack of wisdom as regards health care delivery We who have to bear the brunt of it all. Aren't our kids worth that little risk of an extra day? I, the hospital and yes, you. We may grumble if we find out that our kids aren't affected, but we still would be grateful to know that our best interests are kept in mind.

I wish I could say otherwise, but it feels like a sharp blow to know that the ones into which our lives and futures are being placed in terms of health care are sometimes gullible and uncaring, and some only care about the statistics. When did providing proper health care become synonymous with being cold and unfeeling and completely unable to show empathy? Or to think ahead and sacrifice a little more time and effort to prevent an irreversible state?

The irreversibility of it all is what sometimes makes me feel terrible. Like it really cannot get much better than it currently is, no matter how many interventions we decide to have. In summary, Vasili can never have a normal life again. He is condemned to make the best use of what life has been offered him. Maybe, just maybe, if he'd been born disabled, it wouldn't be so hard to comprehend but the fact that I had seen him so perfect, as yet untainted by the tragedy which was looming around the corner. That fact makes me want to shake myself out of this dreamy state and awaken myself into what was real. Is it really my perfect baby boy who cannot see or hear or walk at the age of 5? It still gets to me, on those bad days and I sometimes wonder what it must feel like for any parent who has to watch this happen to their child. It's gruesome, words can't really describe it... No matter how people say they understand, they can't truly understand. To watch your bundle of beautiful joy become transformed in an instant, due to some negligence and the passing off of a test that would only have cost a pound yet would have saved us all these stressful days, it's gruesome. To deny this young beautiful boy a full and normal existence is heart wrenching.

On those days when I think about it, I would want to break-down, but again, when I imagine his thoughts, the way he still carries on so graciously as little as he is and in spite of all he has been through, I find strength in his strength, I am up-lifted and given another opportunity to try again.

Elena's Diary

It's not an easy day to day life that's for sure, it wasn't anything like what I was use to or what my friends and family were going through with their newborns. I mean there is having sleepless nights or disturbed nights and then there is actual sleep deprivation!! I would be desperate to close my eyes but also so scared to, in case something life threatening would happen to my baby, especially in the early stages. He was very vulnerable, and at this stage I was still learning and understanding him. I would torture myself, researching his condition and endlessly looking for a miracle cure at any chance I would get to educate myself and to help him in any way possible.

I wish the dangers in jaundice were a little more highlighted to parents. After all jaundice is very common. And yes, I understand the professionals don't want to scare parents unnecessarily. While all mothers get big 'bounty' packs thrown at them full of information when you've just had a baby...having three children I've never read anything in those packs highlighting jaundice, only vitamin k which they never tell you that in some cases could be dangerous if given to children with underlining deficiencies.

I've seen huge amounts of information encouraging breastfeeding which I am one hundred percent in agreement with, but you can also have breastfeeding jaundice.

My point is, if the NHS are lacking in qualified staff and training resources and are discharging mothers and babies on the same day of birth, the level of care and monitoring is not as it should be, which on those critical days are when observations should be at its best. Therefore, it's important that the parents are somewhat aware of certain risks factors to look out for.

I've never ever told someone the story of my son and someone tell me they knew jaundice could cause brain damage. This in some way serves me some comfort but also upsets me at the same time.

There are definitely changes which need to be made. Yes, we have been told that there have been changes made in our community but are those changes permanent and will it follow through to new student nurses?

Please don't think I am putting out the blame to innocent midwives, nurses or medical staff, we just need change to prevent this from happening again and again.

Because we know we are not the first or the last, which is shocking in this day and age, there are preventatives there to avoid this type of brain damage from happening. So it's the monitoring which is at fault and knowing when treatment is needed before it's too late.

One terrifying thing which my Spartan faces is the 'locked in' state. That is, apart from the brain areas which have been affected by Kernicterus, many other areas are properly functioning. This means he has the intelligence of a normal child and can live a normal life if allowed, but he is locked in - and he just can't. Have you ever experienced not being able to do something which you would otherwise easily have achieved? It's traumatising. But to know that my baby goes through this every single day? That just knocks me down to my knees when I think about it and also about the obvious fact that there really is nothing I can do about it. I am as helpless, as he is and that hurts severely.

Furthermore, he has had to battle with Spastic Cerebral Palsy which means that when he tries to move, he has certain angulations or twisting of his limbs, his head and even his mouth. His knees are pressed together with his legs and feet turned inwards. His muscles are also very tense and stiff, and he makes a lot of jerky movements. As if to worsen the battle, he also has gastric issues for which he takes medications and also for the Cerebral Palsy. We have a physiotherapist who comes to see him, and he has to take some strings of medications for this also.

Odd enough as it seems, I have truly watched on as Vasili takes on such strength that I have never seen anyone else exhibit. With his exhibition of strength, who am I to refuse to continue to push ahead? I might not like the outcome of events, but the truth is that I have been blessed profusely by these self-same events.

My family might have been through so much pain, but I know that it will get better. I know, that in spite of this, the only way for us, is forward.

Chapter 7:

Healthcare and Finances |

The disability world is very expensive. I do not like to discuss money when it comes to disability, but the truth is the costs of care, support and disability aids are extreme. To think that a one pound test could have prevented this. And yet, certain officials deem this to not be the right way forward, and yet when I see more cases like what happened to my son reoccurring, it truly saddens me every day.

I strongly suggest to anyone, to have in place some kind of healthcare insurance for their loved ones; you simply do not know what is around the corner.

It is indeed painful to watch one's dreams, ambitions and aspirations come to naught because of a medical illness in the life of a loved one. This includes our whole family to some extent, but we aim to change this as we will not be pigeon-holed as the "the disabled family", we'd rather be known as the family that took on the adversity and turned it into a humbled positivity.

Sometimes, I think it is those who have the burden of providing healthcare in a condition where it has to be an out-of-pocket payment that suffer the most when a loved one is ill, not necessarily the loved one himself.

This is not to trivialise the pain felt by sick individuals, but to point out the severe pain of watching a child, parent, brother, sister or friend, deal with a chronic illness, especially when it seems as if hope is getting progressively lost, and yet having to source for funds to take care of this individual, regardless. How do you think or even talk about doing other important things like paying household bills when your child is billed for a major surgery? How can you think about payment of fees for your other children? What about the pretty important matters of feeding other members of the family? How is the family able to function properly in the presence of such dire situations?

I am moved with compassion and a strong understanding of how this affects parents and health care givers and because of this we plan to set up a fund, a charity organisation to help Vasili and other children. This will happen, and my aim is that by the time I clock 45 years of age, I would have achieved this. Goal setting is extremely important but it's equally important to work on a realistic goal and not to be disheartened if things do not go according to plan. The main concept is to move forward and not backward and to move at a trajectory that is more inclined than levelled. This way, we grow no matter what. This has been my journey. With consistent sleep deprivation, I have been able to go into property investing, marketing and design projects for clients and I have had to adapt to this paucity of sleep. Some have questioned me, saying, "how do you do it?" My response is that my son shows me the way as do my other children. The fact is that any one is capable of anything. To find the time and energy is hard when you are faced with a lot of physical pressures, but I have learnt that they are not impossible, and they can be achieved. If the right percentage of focus is used, the compound effect of all your efforts will result in the achievement of great rewards.

Miracle and Funds

Some friends over the years have kindly set up fund raisers to help my son with additional experiences and tools that aid him. For this we are eternally grateful, and there have been many people (they know themselves). I would like to thank them dearly for their contribution towards Vasili's fund. Apart from the gifts received, there is this strength which comes when one knows that there are people who truly care about him and are willing to provide support for him in trying times. When you feel alone and exhausted, it is amazing how a stranger's love for your son can lift your spirits. It is a beautiful sight to visualise love flowing directly from the heart of one human be-ing, and to see my son's face light up and glow on receiving this. I truly believe my son accepts their positive energy and that it helps him and makes him stronger. I know that must sound weird, but I have seen it and it's true.

Take for instance when, not many months ago, my son had a follow-up test on his sight. My wife and I had been dreading this, as we had been told that he was totally blind. But we knew that there was more to his sight, owing to the fact that he just seemed to be much more aware than what the "experts" were saying. Anyway, the test took some time and involved placing some probes on my son's head and monitoring them as they placed a monitor in front of him and played some video. Well, we had the results and the doctors had been surprised as were we. His sight was deemed normal!! "How is this possible?" we asked. There was no way of explaining this, as the condition that caused his blindness in essence had stained the nerves to his eyes and so his eyes were functional, but there was no communication between his brain and his eyes. In the early years prior to finding this result, we had searched high and low for ways that could help our son as we could not bear the thought of him never being able to see us. We stumbled across a therapy from America by a lady called Dr. Christine Roman who specialised in a light therapy treatment that basically involved sitting in a dark place with my son and shining a tungsten torch in his eyes until the pupils would change size, and then switching the torch on and off. We would repeatedly do this, taking turns between my wife and myself for the first year. It was in essence massaging the nerves to reawaken the ones that may still be there or that were partially damaged. It was also used to help stimulate new growth and nerve endings. In the beginning my son would not flinch, up until one day which was 5 months after we had started doing this. I was sitting with him at 3:40 am and I was doing the light treatment with him. On the 7th time, he flinched slightly and closed his eyes. I did not think much of this response, as I was used to having no response from him, so I did it again and he flinched in response to the light. Some days later, my wife also noticed the same. We knew that he was still classified as blind, but he could see light! We were so happy because it was a start and the start to our newfound hope.

It's amazing how much we have spent on extra stimuli over the past 5 years, and if I had to sum it all up, I think I would send myself swirling, so I would rather not. I should be keeping and recording our expenses more, but I just want to live a normal life as best as can be. At the same time, I have also provided aid and given to other families struggling with similar conditions. At some point, I was paying from debt on my card but there is some kind of bigger pain that drives you when you experience the same or something similar to those you can relate to. We enjoy helping as much as we can as a family, and the sense of fulfilment gained from doing this in the recent years is immense. I knew that I had to focus on my own family when funds started to be a problem especially with my own job being affected by the new world we were living.

With costs being high for families in similar situations, I would suggest one very potent way in which we have been able to reduce these healthcare costs, especially as regards to physical therapy, and this is by using whatever little measures we can utilise at home, such as engaging in exercises which are good for him. With that, we have been able to cut back on some of the cost, and sometimes we don't realise just how much we can save by taking this approach. You might not know it at the time, but eventually it does add up to something big. I tend to not tally up and I hate making our lives dependent on this, but I do not splash out on things that are unnecessary, just because there may be funding for it from our healthcare service. I feel it's important to have a fair balance for the system we all use. This does not negate the fact that due to the severity of his disability, he does cost a lot to care for and we have caregivers and a disability van paid for, which I sincerely appreciate. However, I cannot be fully grateful knowing that he was born healthy and this was not his own doing. My gratitude comes from those maimed in other countries and who do not have such support.

Even with all the cut backs and unfair decisions, I still am very grateful for our NHS and the good people that reside and work ever so hard within it.

So, if you are struggling with any healthcare support for your child or any other loved one, I would suggest that you become their personal 'at home therapist' and to effectively do this, you might need to learn techniques, which might prove to be beneficial for them. Besides the health benefits, your undertaking to apply the massage on your child leads to more bonding, you and your child can share the experience together, trust is maintained, love is encouraged, and infinite bonding occurs.

We were the therapists and masseurs. We already embraced the culture of massaging Vasili's feet and limbs, his neck region and his back. We have read several books and conducted a lot of researches, many of which have helped us. We would also use hydrotherapy not just purely for enjoyment but for tension relief. The effects it has on his body for at least twenty hours later is incredible and so satisfying to see some relief in his muscles. The therapy was encouraged by school and other therapists as they also witnessed the great benefits. Remember the torch thing I mentioned earlier? Yes, we do a lot of other therapeutic treatment just so he can become better, improving upon himself, and even us, in the process.

We would try exercising together, helping him to move his limbs. And it's been fun, really. Countless times, we have seen that face he makes when he wants his body exercised. It has helped us to bond greatly with him too. He has come to adjust with our way of moving and I'm very glad about that. It's very necessary to try one's possible best to be actively involved in the treatment of the child, no matter in what dimension it is being carried out.

It would also be best if you could stay very much involved in your child's healthcare because then, you would know what is being tried and why it is being tried. It makes you less likely to complain so much about his healthcare, since now you know that his doctors, nurses, physiotherapists; and other members of the health care team are trying their best to ensure he attains the highest possible health that he could.

However, I would still like to talk about funding when it comes to health care options such as surgeries, which he has to undergo, and which are indeed in his best interest. Shouldn't such interventions be free, seeing as this condition, in the first place, was caused by negligence? Like I said earlier, I am not trying to apportion blame, I am only stating the facts. Yes, we get provisions, well the standard provisions he is due as a higher rate disabled child, but what about leading treatments abroad - why do families like ours have to fund to seek specialists in distant countries? This is often the case not just in these situations, but also for ill health patients. For instance, having to sell their homes to stay alive only for a few more weeks because the costs are huge. I know the truth and that's if we are to face the realities of the situation, it would be too expensive for us alone to bear this very heavy burden. Even more so, that this was certainly no fault of Vasili nor was any fault of ours, and yet we have to shoulder it and live with it. Sometimes it may seem as though we are not doing enough but I am unsure I will ever feel satisfied with the amount of help I can give to my son or my family. I'm sure as a parent we all feel we can never do enough and always strive to give more.

For now, there is no cure. But, we are never saying never. And I plan to be ready for when there comes a time he will have the support he so deserves. My dream is to see him grow old and improve to keep improving, reaching more milestones. I hope we can grow old ourselves as even at forty years old, I have aged immensely, and I know, if I am to be realistic, my body will worsen with age and caring for my beloved son would become harder...

Let us examine this from a purely sincere point of view, is it ethically correct for us to pay for a condition which occurred due to lack of proficiency on the part of the NHS which allowed a student midwife to attend to my son unaccompanied? I really do not think so. I think here you may assume I am talking about my son's condition, well no..... I am talking of my family's condition whilst my son has care costs covered. Our freedom and work choices and the ability to earn as we had in the past have been obliterated. This is another example of one of the tentacles of the problems families like ours face. The multiplier effect of having to deal with a situation like this and yet people assume we are provided for in these circumstances, like we get some kind of lottery pay out. It does not work like that. And believe me, I would rather live in a shed and have my son and his health back than any monetary compensation for us personally. I fear for when we are not here for the future of my kids, as they have additional challenges. So I am on the route to creating this one way or another; I will do it so watch this space.

Funding this illness has drained my family's account and although we love Vasili, his health care has taken much more from us than we would be able to even recount. Although funding has been difficult, we have tried to ensure that Vasili has everything that he needs. But still, it has been an uphill struggle and we wake up every day knowing that the battle continues. You see, the cost of bringing up my son is increased by the fact that my very freedom to be able to work a regular job has been taken away from me. I mean, I appreciate the fact that we have a health care system and any support we get also. But we don't get support for our loss, how our holidays and our freedom are affected. How we now live in a home with strangers, when we have caregivers, that is. It's a new existence of catch twenty-two; you don't win. It's a loss-loss scenario. And when it comes down to freedoms of this sort, we are left high and dry with absolutely no choice.

Thankfully, we have a solicitor who is in charge of our family estate and so we don't have to figure this out on our own, but with the aid of a qualified professional.

My heart goes out to all the parents out there, who have children with Kernicterus, Cerebral Palsy or any other chronic debilitating illness and worse, those who do not have access to any form of health insurance policy. Knowing how much we struggle, even with insurance, it must be hell to live without insurance. I might not know so much, or might not be in your shoes, but I certainly know that it's very hard.

There are however, a couple of things which can be done in the home setting such as beneficial exercise, increasing the activity level of your child and ensuring that even if he or she cannot attain the same level of physical activity as the other children, you don't limit what level can be attained because of fear. I must admit that this is one area I am still struggling with,

101

because I have protected Vasili since birth. I feel like I am obligated to continue to protect him, but know that I cannot do so forever.

Being active, I have noticed, has particularly helped to reduce some of the spasms which Vasili has experienced over time, and I am very glad to see such glaringly positive changes!

Sometimes, when the chips are down, it isn't just money that is required, but mostly it is love which enables you to try many interventions that can be helpful. And eventually, help our loved ones to achieve such strength as we have known to be possible, yet we are very much afraid to believe that they could attain.

Illness is painful in all the ways possible. be it psychologically, physically, mentally, emotionally as well as financially. I sincerely think that the cost of healthcare should be really looked into and revamped. Money always seems to be the elephant in the room which everyone tries to ignore, but which we all know is important. Health is also important and as such, people would pay as much money as is required to be healthy- even to the point of having nothing else left.

I can't begin to dissect the strong impact which Vasili's illness has had on his elder sister in particular, as regards to things which we ought to get done for her. I am deeply pained when Ellie ought to get the full attention she so deserves, or we are supposed to give her an experience which she really deserves. That is made impossible due to circumstances beyond our control and which have caused, or rather, put us in a place where we literally cannot do as much as we would have done because our hands are tied by our position. This has been the case more often than I would care to admit.

Have you ever heard that one of the most common reasons for divorce and other related conflicts in marriage is money? That's pretty right. We make quite a sum of money, between Elena and I but most of it goes to healthcare provision for our awesome son, treatments that are not covered by the insurance. Now, any one parent could have chosen to leave at any point because this wasn't exactly what she was subscribing for when she married me, no one subscribes to a lifetime of pain and sickness. Yet I must commend her level of strength and courage, her consistent desire to see that our son gets the best possible care and becomes as healthy as he can be. That quality is one which I respect deeply and if I had to trade her for any other woman in the world, I simply would not. She was, and still is, my gem, my rock, I wouldn't have been able to see it through this far if it wasn't for her and the kids. I repeat I wouldn't trade her for anything, any day!

She has been a source of encouragement not only to me, her husband, but for a lot of Women at PICK, and also at several other places where we meet people that find out about our child's condition. Many are even more awed when they realise only after several months, that Vasili is the way he is. They say that whenever they hear her talk about her baby, that they never for once imagined it. She goes about her daily activities just as every other mother would, never appearing weak. No, she isn't weak. I know that at times, especially at the beginning, it's challenging. But you don't see her relate with people like others would have done, painting it as if they have upon their shoulders, the burden of the whole world.

She's always on her feet, ready to volunteer to do some work or carry out projects which would later on receive accolades. She doesn't allow anyone around her to be down. As she is trying to ensure that Ellie doesn't feel left out of the whole attention thing, she is taking care of Vasili in such a way that he doesn't feel that he is getting all of the care because he is not living up to expectation. She knows just how to handle the whole situation around the house. She doesn't live like the women who wear the same shoes as her. I see her gather a few of them, speaking to them. In fact, she gets a number of calls from different women across the world. One recommendation to another, and she is changing lives. Sincerely, I still astonished at her aura and grace which exudes hard work, diligence, love, commitment, confidence and you name it. My superhero.

Elena's Diary

Learn to say no! Having a newborn baby is difficult at first, especially until you have recovered from labour but having a newborn and dealing with a whole new world of disability was even more challenging! Using medical terms I had never heard of before and finding my way around most departments of the hospital was alien. It felt like I was walking along corridors of a death sentence. On my most depressing days, when I never wanted to step another foot in that hospital, but did knowing I had no choice. My son was at their mercy, I would be lacking in answers to tests my son had to torturously take. I had countless appointments every day of the week. So the first thing I had to do was get myself a diary to schedule all of his appointments. The second thing I did was buy a filing cabinet to store all of his appointment letters and reports from the hospital. I was rushing myself and my children to one appointment after the next.... my daughter spending most of her days in these depressing walls. I tried my best to make it as fun as possible on our journeys and taking toys along with us. At the end of the day she was happy just being with her family. But it was far from what we both had envisaged with a new edition to the family.

We started a campaign to raise awareness and our amazing family all came together to create a fantastic charity event. But we wanted more than that. We wanted to make a difference by raising more awareness. We had meetings with the patient safety team in London, we wrote to the House of Commons to fight for Kernicterus on the Never Events list as it is in America, we had calls from magazines and BBC news for several interviews and radio interviews. We were running dry on energy and clinging onto hope, all at the same time as we were recruiting and managing carers at home which was a full-time job in itself. Then I learnt to say no, enough was enough. I realised I wanted answers from every professional I met but I soon came to realise that many times I was in fact educating them about Kernicterus and that they were learning from Vasili... Kernicterus is not a term many professionals know of, Cerebral Palsy yes, deaf yes, blind yes, but Kernicterus not so commonly known. I would travel far to many different hospitals for many reasons which was distressing for Vasili and for myself. When you have had barely any sleep and then travelling around on little resources I began to turn down appointments which I knew Vasili wouldn't benefit from. I filtered them out and soon life became calmer and we all had so much more time to focus on his therapy and care at home, whilst my daughter was in her favourite environment. There was less stress and pressure on myself, so it was a win-win! Life was now more precious than ever before, and I didn't want to waste any of it.

Chapter 8:

Forgiveness |

As I type that word, I feel a mix of emotions running through me. Why would I forgive, or rather, why would my family choose to forgive the NHS when so much pain and damage has been caused? Why would we rather let go of this when it has caused us irreparable damage?

Make no mistake, we are very hurt. However, for us, blaming is not the way forward without some kind of change to improve the system. If I had the opportunity to have a heart-to-heart discussion with the 'powers that be' in that sector, I would totally utilise this opportunity and for me, this is definitely more productive than blaming them. If the healthcare system had been better, none of the things that came to happen to us would have been experienced. It is particularly painful that it was something so preventable, and was considered an act of negligence that has led up to this.

Several times a day, I ask myself certain questions. What if our son's bilirubin level had been checked? What if that had not been overlooked? What if the very first midwife that came had alerted us that there was a possibility of something more severe going on, instead of just reassuring us about it being not a serious occurrence all of the time? What if she had not generalised but instead, had been specific about our son, instead of focusing on my wife and barely taking a look at my son? Was it that the training which she and others like her had received made it so easy to generalise occurrences amongst children and other sick individuals? Why had the second midwife not been urgent? In fact, why had we even been discharged without the doctors adequately checking all parameters inclusive of serum bilirubin levels, even though we had stayed in the hospital for much longer due to Elena's desire to have some calm before going home, thus removing any case of it being related to there being no time to screen him?

Although we have made the decision to forgive and to move on, it is immensely difficult, I must confess. How do we get over the fact that our son could have been able to jump, skip and play around just like his elder sister and other friends of his age? Each time I see a child who is about the same age as he is, it is very hard for me not to break down into tears, understandably. I love Vasili very much and even in his state, I am greatly inspired, but it is very difficult for me to get it out of my mind that he was born as a healthy child.

However, even if we forgive, the NHS still needs to recognise how much work is needed to ensure that everyone is treated with utmost regard, and that each preventable illness is, indeed, prevented.

There ought to be strategies put in place to ensure that each healthcare provider has rules which makes him or her responsible for carrying out necessary tests and for doing all the essential tasks. Apart from that, there has to be strict rules put in place for defaulters, so as to prevent this from happening to other children. Although I am speaking up about our pain, I sadly know that my family has not been the first to have experienced this sort of pain. There are countless other children suffering from Kernicterus, which in the first place, could have been prevented. Many of them are either too sorrowful to relieve the pain and choose to just bury it in their minds, while many don't even have the luxury of time to talk about the incidence. As a matter of fact, I wouldn't be surprised if many a parent or sibling has gone into severe depression on the basis of this kind of occurrence, as we did, for in these events, it is the relatives of the sick person that are most severely hit in the face by it. They often bear the most brunt of the impact of such conditions to the life of the sufferer as well as the disruption to their own life cycle. All of life's activities seem to come to a standstill in the face of severe illness in a loved one's life. How is life supposed to even go on?

But this is the simple truth; that life has to go on. By experience, I know that being stuck in the past does very little, if anything at all, to help anyone. It only affords you the opportunity of wallowing in the pain of the past and of ruminating events and how things could have been different or better, how things could have gone on differently.

For example, I have wondered if Vasili would have had Kernicterus if he had been born in an up-to-date, state-of-the-art facility. Would he have developed this preventable spectrum of illnesses if he had been born in a facility where everything was done properly and according to the book, where nothing was overlooked? This is a wake-up call to the healthcare industry, for these local institutions to be developed into state-of-the- art institutions, where things are done as they ought to be done.

For the Kalisperas family, we have decided to see whatever joy we can in this situation and instead of blaming someone, to use this as an avenue to encourage other parents in the self-same situation as we are, or similar situations. It is our utmost desire that they would find strength in this seeming desolation and would gather the courage, and if possible borrow from our experience and the life lessons that Vasili teaches us to get back on your two feet and stand tall in the face of whatever adversity that comes around. The fact remains, that there is so much more to live for, even if you were to consider that there was almost nothing to live for. Look to the young child, appreciate the sheer strength and courage they have shown through all of the challenges that life has thrown at them, see how they remain resolute and draw courage from it, for yourself and for the other siblings and family members if there are any.

We also use this avenue to reach out to the authorities to ensure that things are properly done and that these workers in the healthcare service institutions have the appropriate training and are properly equipped to carry out the needed tasks. Also, a student should never be asked to do something so life endangering without supervision. I totally understand how, without practice, a student midwife or doctor cannot become proficient, but this shouldn't be to the detriment of the one who is to receive care. In future, I hope such avenues for which mistakes can be so readily made are scrapped out of the system, because this can only facilitate more and more errors and make people condemn the system or even institute cases in the legal courts.

We have chosen the higher way. We have chosen the path of forgiveness. It doesn't make dealing with the situation any easier, but it certainly does help moving on become a little easier.

Chapter 9:

MBH |

To those of you that do not believe in miracles, OPEN YOUR MINDS, as I've witnessed many. My son struggles to have control over his body due to the Cerebral Palsy. His muscles are always contracting, his body fighting Quadriplegic Spastic Cerebral Palsy, Although being blind, deaf and cannot speak, he does verbalise and communicate in his own way.

I clearly remember the sheer happiness in my soul when I read the best message from my wife. She had sent me videos of my son at his conductive education centre, where he attends regularly. The videos may have not looked like much to some but to me it was amazing.

I just couldn't believe it! How is this possible?!

He is weight bearing and is progressing into taking steps and controlling his body so much more, fantastic head control and sitting unaided, four-point kneeling unaided... I just couldn't believe the miracles before my eyes.

When I was working I would often find myself crying in the work toilet, trying to hold my despair as I watched families walk in with their healthy children. It was hard to see and to know it was preventable and that my son was born healthy.

A lady walked into where I was working at the time, she had a particular warmth about her and she was showing interest in my conversation I was in with another customer at the time. I eventually spoke to her of our heartache. Yes, not professional, but I felt comfortable speaking to this lady.

Then the lady asked if I knew that she worked at a certain disability establishment. I had no idea what that meant, it turned out it was a very respected, charitable, disability rehabilitation centre for children with disabilities of many types.

Not just anyone could enroll, as it is application based only., They had limited resources and are highly sought after from families across the world. This place was only a few miles from where we lived also, and the lovely lady asked me to send an application through.

Well that's where it all started, I believe this was pure fate and the universe working for us and I owe a lot to her and her team. These miracles and advances are also due to her amazing team at the centre. We love that special place and so does Vasili. This incredible healing centre has been the only place where we have felt so much hope, believing my son can reach his goals with so much strength and consistency... Perseverance really does pay off.

Our Third Child

Although this book is really about Vasili, I would like to touch on the subject of the youngest member of our family, one who has also added much warmth and love to our family in spite of all we are going through. It is indeed, very amazing to note where we learnt the most lessons in life. Once again, one of my children has taught me a very practicable lesson, one which is useful in so many life situations. Indeed, I have been blessed and that is how I would always want to view my life and family; as rare a blessing which we couldn't have given to ourselves, by ourselves.

She was born out of love. Seeing as I am someone who tends to monitor my wife's pregnancies, I certainly monitored this one even more carefully.

Vasili was just a little over 2 years of age when we had another baby on the way. This time, my wife was neither depressed nor boisterous. She was instead, a calmer version of herself, a calmer version of the woman whom I had married some 5 years ago.

I helped around the house pretty often, and now that we had gotten used to Vasili's ailments, we had sort of formed a routine of taking care of him, and his elder sister whilst also ensuring the other household chores were not left unattended.

We still tried to stay in love, but this time, it was a seemingly more mature form of love. We loved, but it certainly couldn't compare to how we were as newlyweds. I for one, wished we could have been as before, but I knew it was wishful thinking. It was gone, and gone forever. Who knows, maybe we could desire a fourth child, I thought amusingly to myself. I didn't dare to mention it to my wife, she wouldn't have seen the funny side to it after all that she had been through.

Those 9 months, we tried to ensure Elena got as much rest as she needed, well, as much as she could get with the fact that we were incessantly worried about Vasili, but for most of the time, she was fine.

The truth is Elena suffered a lot during this pregnancy, she suffered extremely with her back from carrying the weight of our unborn and the constant weight of carrying Vasili began to take its toll. She had constant infections, she had the stress of undergoing Vasilis cochlear implants operation and recovery. Vasili was in hospital with severe gastroenteritis so she was constantly worried she would miscarry due to the stress she was under. I don't know how she did it to be honest, but with strength and love, we pulled through together as much as we could to keep strong. She had constant appointments with a consultant to make sure everything was okay with the baby, we had more scans than usual just for reassurance.

Elena was always afraid of having an emergency Caesarean section, but this time she had requested to have one so that she could plan care for Vasili and Ellie and know which date the new baby would arrive in this world. Funny enough, Maria was due on the exact same day as my eldest daughter Ellie. Elena decided to make their birthdays at least a day apart, to let them each have their own special day, so Maria was born the day before Ellie - which was the best birthday present we could have ever given her!

A tour was suggested by one of the nurses to help Elena feel more comfortable on the day of giving birth, and to attempt seeing the labour rooms once again in case there was to be any chance of a natural birth. As soon as those double doors opened onto the maternity ward, she looked down that corridor and broke down, she couldn't walk any further. She knew the labour room she was in with Vasili was just at the end of the corridor and to see that bath again from the water birth would just make her relive the whole event. She just couldn't face it, it was all too soon and felt so raw. Poor Elena was traumatised. So we went ahead with the original plan of a c-section, it wasn't the ideal situation but we had accepted it was the safest way our baby would enter into the world. She was monitored throughout the whole birth/surgery by our top consultant who had been through everything with us and Vasili, and who we fully trusted.

We were on high alert as you can imagine, for jaundice and straight away, the day after Maria was born Elena noted jaundice in the whites of Maria's eyes! We called upon our trusted consultant and alarm bells began to ring, Elena and I felt like we were reliving our worst fears. This dreaded jaundiced couldn't be happening again.

The paediatrician took a heel prick to measure Maria's jaundiced levels and Elena stayed in hospital for a very long time. We monitored Maria's jaundice over the days of Elena's stay but it kept creeping up. We were frantic as we couldn't risk any brain damage once again, it got to the point where the jaundice carried on rising when it should have been coming down, so we had to demand phototherapy to prevent any damage. She had breast feeding jaundice, so although Elena wanted to breast feed she had no choice but to stop. We compromised on a biliblanket, which was a less intrusive way of lowering the jaundice levels. Soon enough we were home.

When she was born, I started thinking more along the lines of: What if we are supposed to minister to people who had disabled children? Was there more to our lives than we knew? What was our calling as a family, and were we given the strength to bear all of this with so much fortitude because there was something greater, more inspirational which our pain was supposed to achieve?

Maybe God wanted us to have the practical experience of living with a child with disability so we would truly understand and grow into really strong people. Then, we might have more insight and emphatically understand parents of disabled children more. Sure enough, it is easier for us to empathise and not just to sympathise with other parents in similar conditions, especially since we decided to forgive the NHS and free up the space which bitterness had previously occupied in our hearts.

Indeed, we have begun to work more on this, and although it wasn't entirely easy for us to handle, we have grown to appreciate them all, to celebrate their little successes, and laugh at the beauty that life has afforded us, daily. Today, when I think about my family and how many hurdles we have faced in terms of disability, I can boldly say that I appreciate my family, and, in fact, I wouldn't have had it any other way. We have been bonded by pain, strengthened by sorrow, cried together and laughed at the little progress each of us has made together. Together, we have built a formidable little team of individuals who cannot be broken by pain, finally coming to a point where we are strong enough to inspire others and strengthen those who faint or are sorrowful around us, just by them looking at us and observing our abilities to smile through pain. This impact in itself is one of our successes. The sheer thought that we stand as inspiration to someone out there who is going through the same challenge or something far greater, that they can look to us and draw inspiration and strength from the way we have been able to manage and continue to carry on in dignity.

I have come to the realisation in life, that it isn't those with the least amount of problems that are the happiest, rather it is those who appreciate every little progress that they make, those who have chosen to see the joy in pain, to see the strength and abilities in their places of weakness. Without my children, I would never have learnt all of these lessons or grown into such a strong man that I am today. I would still be immature and probably taking out everything which life hands out to me with laxity, not having learnt how to fight back and win even in the face of hopelessness.

Besides the pain which Vasili goes through daily, I have learnt this: life might hand out terrible situations to you and make you feel as though there is no way out, but if you choose to see the good in every situation, then you would surmount those obstacles. If you choose to see yourself as a fighter and a winner, that is exactly whom you would become - one who fights and wins; just like our precious children.

For most winners, winning isn't some great trait which they were born with, or which only they have a special gene for winning. But rather, it was something which they chose to develop in spite of all the odds. Now, I see the ability to win as a character trait which can help one fight all odds and come out victorious. In summary, I wouldn't forget our baby for teaching me how to break barriers, to overlook, self-imposed or otherwise, limits. My son had been given a doctor-imposed limit of only a few months at most, yet he broke through that barrier, tore that label off himself as though it were nothing. Usually, as we grow older and meet with disappointments, it becomes increasingly harder to tear off limitations because we have gotten used to them. However, it is definitely worth it, and as soon as any limitation is being imposed on you, I challenge you to tear it off, to make it known to everyone else that you would not be bound by any external force, but instead, you will achieve all that you have been programmed, destined, to achieve. That is the character trait of a winner, and I firmly believe that we all can be winners! We all can break those self-imposed and otherwise limits. We all can get to a point where regardless of the external environment, all we keep on doing is soar far above those limitations, and that we have an inability to be limited by anything at all within our environment.

My eldest daughter Ellie, who was only four years old at the time when Vasili was born, had taken to our new routine quite well. As she was so young at the time, she didn't really take any notice of playing in the neonatal unit every evening as we tried our best to keep her entertained. Life was being over taken with appointments and care for Vasili, that she definitely wasn't receiving the attention she was used to. She was having more sleep overs at grandparents and relatives than usual, but she didn't mind that. She was always an artistic little girl. She had mature drawing skills from a very young age, and she would draw beautiful tree houses and happy thoughts. Then her drawings began to change their theme, into ears, syringes, eyes, finger pricking, from constantly watching the nurses take Vasili's blood, and worry about his hearing loss and eyesight. I tried my best to relay her fears, but I called upon a play specialist which was part of the open access we had to the children's ward. She used play to express any fears or feelings she was experiencing. She drew a picture of worries and they all included worries of Vasili's operations, wishing his eye sight would come back, worries about her first day at school which was the same day as his operation.

She then wrote a story of "once upon a time, there was a mum and a dad who had a little baby, he got really poorly and needed to go to hospital, he had an injection which made him better and they all lived happily ever after". Her pictures were detailed of the hospital and the ambulances parked outside. When I read it, I burst into tears and my heart hurt. I just wanted to protect her so much. After a few more sessions it did help her speaking to someone unrelated to the event and have some dedicated time.

She sometimes attends sibling groups at a hospice, where she can meet and relate with other siblings who have been through trauma.

Ellie has written a short story of how she remembers things...

I can barely remember Vasili as a baby as I was only four when he was born, but when I look back at pictures I start to remember little things. I think the biggest memory I have is when my mum came back home with him, I was expecting a girl and I was actually a little sad that I didn't have a little sister, but I was still over the moon I had a sibling, a new best friend.

I just remember running downstairs shouting "is it a girl"? Vasili was supposed to come home on a Saturday morning but instead he came home on Friday night. I was SO excited to be having a baby brother or sister and I even remember the dream I had the night before.

This is how I remember it;

My mum wakes me up (I know she wouldn't normally do that on a Saturday) she says "Ellie, why don't you come and see your new baby sister"

Then I ask her "where is she?" And she tells me "downstairs in the living room" as I was walking down the stairs to see my baby sister, I trip over on the step and then I woke up from my sleep.

I was six years old when I found out that Vasili was disabled and I was REALLY sad then. Vasili was one when he had his first cochlear implant and I was really quite scared for him. That very day, it was my first ever day of primary school and I couldn't stop thinking of Vasili. He wasn't disabled all of his life though, he had jaundice very badly and all because of this he is now disabled. We call him our little spartan now, because he is so strong, and even our priest at church says he is our ticket to heaven. Vasili was two years old when he had his second cochlear implant and at first it was too loud for him, but now he's used to it.

And then my wish came true, I now also had a little sister Maria! I finally had someone that I could run around with, I was so happy! I love playing with my little sister and I also have found many fun ways to play with my brother too, he is so cute and I love to make him laugh! He has a beautiful smile.

I think my little spartan is: Adorable, brave, just AMAZING, loveable and our little spartan!! Vasili is my little brother, he is cute, loveable and fun to play with and here are some poems of mine:

My Little Brother

His name is Vasili not silly

I bet he would love to properly play

He would put on his shoes and run around all day

When he came in, he would kick me in the shin and

shout hip hip hooray!

About Vasili

Me

I am 5

I can't dive

I love to eat, I share

But I shall tell you what I really can't bear

My tube!

It's stuck in my tummy,

Where my lovely mummy and carers put in water, med-
icine and food

But I like to taste my food not just to be full and when

Sometimes people put in just too much!

I go..... Blurp!!!

Sound

C-R-A-C-K-L-E-C-R-A-C-K

-I- H-E-A-R -R-O-B-O-T-I-C S-O-U-N-D-S- -I-

H-A-T-E -I-T-

CCCCCCCCRRRRRRAAAAACCCCKKK   BOOM
CRACK SMACK BANG

WHAT'S HAPPENED?
Oh great, has my cochlear fallen off? WHY?
DID THE BATTERY DIE?
MAYBE IT WAS FROM WHEN I MOVED TO THE
SIDE THE MAGNET SLIPPED OFF
AND THAT HAPPENS A LOT!

Chapter 10:

Wrapping it up - Strength in The Midst of Severe Pain and Hopelessness |

There is a certain variety of pain which is hinged on the knowledge of the fact that what had caused the pain was indeed, very preventable. It is pretty numbing to discover that if things hadn't played out the way they had, you wouldn't be in the place you were today.

As with Vasili's case, I'm pretty sure that anyone in a similar situation would replay the events over and over again in their heads, what if this had happened instead of that? What if I had done this, or hadn't done that?

And sometimes, it is very hard to move on from that spot- in fact, you come to that spot in your mind every day, checking to see if it's still there and you ask yourself that same question, bothering on why it happened the way it did and what role you and everyone else had played, indeed, apportioning blame to whom it was deserved.

It is particularly hard, and my family and I know all too well, the feeling of helplessness that comes when you know that something could have been done, but wasn't.

This is to encourage anyone who is facing any such situation, and to nudge you gently in the direction of letting go of that time and that situation, be it a disability, the death of a loved one, any predicament which has befallen you and which you feel could have been prevented if picked up on early enough, or if you yourself or someone else had intervened soon enough.

In every pain, there is a lesson. And you might say 'Oh, you can say that because you have found joy somehow in your situation, but I haven't because my case is even worse off!'

Which is why I told you about how messed up I was only a few years earlier. Less than four years ago, I could never have even thought of sharing what I know, seeing that I was dealing with depression, obesity and a host of other medical conditions. But you know what? The fact that I am here today, alive and happily enjoying my perfect family, is proof enough that you can also make it out of that situation.

And though it might not look like it, there is light at the end of your tunnel and at the risk of saying this too much: There is purpose in your pain!

How do I find this purpose in this seemingly endless abyss of pain, you ask?

First, you'd have to accept the situation. It has happened, your son is paralysed, your husband or wife has passed away. You need to get out of denial, out of the shock that unravelled you when you got wind of that piece of life changing news. You need to, absolutely need to, stop playing those scenes in your head with the aim of deleting the deleterious events and replacing them with corrected versions of positive events which would have resulted in a better outcome, at least, from your perspective.

Yes, it could have been avoided, but now that it wasn't, the next thing to do is to look ahead and refuse to live in the past, regretting all of the things that went wrong.

Fling off those coats of weariness and begin to find the joy embedded in your pain.

Vasili has brought us so much joy over the past 5 years that many times I have had to thank God for bringing him into our family. This is not to deny the obvious fact that we shuttle between the hospital and the home ever so frequently, but the smile on his face, when he does smile, is so heavenly.

And I absolutely know, that there is so much more of him to be unravelled as the years roll by and for that, I am very excited. A man walked up to us one day, handed an envelope to us, saying that it was for Vasili. I thanked him for the delivery, but couldn't wait until he was gone to see its content. Immediately we got to the car, before my wife finished her sentence that I should check what was in the envelope, I had torn it open. It was money. I checked the back of the envelope again to see the return address, but there was not one on it. Proving my assumption, it was a gift from the man, to our Spartan. There was a note with the inscription, "for your little boy, I hope he gets to read this by himself one day".

Vasili has touched many lives, although he has had to do multiple surgeries, which aren't even the end of the road, his jumping through all of these hoops shows such an innate resilience, that it gives me hope and strength.

Another blessing that Vasili's life has honoured me with is the grace to meet with so many parents from across the globe on social media platforms and to hear what others are going through. To give as much support as I can, as well as also getting support from certain support groups. I have been opened up to another realm of love which I have enjoyed thoroughly from the early days of Vasili's illness.

Which brings me to ask you, if you have had to deal with traumatic experiences, where do you receive support from? I was never the type of guy who was into the whole support group thing, but I must attest to the fact that they are indeed, very helpful and I would advise that you find one. There is only one caveat, you may need to get the support for yourself in the first place as was our case, when once again support was slow to become available, we had to buckle up and seek support for ourselves and we ended up paying for private support to help us get through our painful thoughts. Once we had it though, we gained so much help and relief as we started to better engage our thoughts and found ways to channel our hurt and pain to positives. Though maybe we may not have fully risen from our ashes like the proverbial phoenix, but I know that we are getting there... the road may be tough sometimes, but it no longer means that it will take away our joy like it did in the early periods of his ailment. We are stronger today in part because of the support we were able to receive, both professionally, from friends and family, and the various support groups and people with shared situations that we have met on this daunting, yet wonderful journey. They have, in one way or another, helped to make the burden of this journey lighter. And I must say that having shared, I and Elena have been able to find succour.

Being a second generation Greek Cypriot like myself, I was instilled from birth that there is no need for counselling and such wishy-washy kind of treatments. You should just dust yourself off and get on with things. There is some truth in this thought, yet it is still too simple to assume it works with the deepest pains of all the problems in the world; that would be silly. My wife and I have made it a point of duty to go for counselling sessions, and we have discovered that it has boosted our communication skills, and besides the fact that it helps us to understand our kids better and take care of them well, it has also strengthened our marriage. One stone to kill two birds, right?

There is a stronger variety of resilience which is only grown by tribulations and watered by more problems, but when we get to the other side, we become witnesses of the possibilities of eliminating problems and creating solutions which work. Pressure makes a man stronger, and I have found that to be immensely true in my life.

I have seen in my boy's eyes, quiet strength and hope, that one day, all of this would be over. Sometimes, I think he is trying to pass across that message of hope to all who come his way, because most people who see him tend to be filled with pity because he doesn't get to live a somewhat "normal" life. But do you know why he is a Spartan? Because in the midst of all of this pain, he doesn't display any attempt at giving up. Instead, he always seems to be actively interested in making people know that when there is life, there is hope.

Severe pain can either be disabling or strengthening and you get to choose what it will be to you, for to one man it may be crippling while to another, it is the stepping stone needed to spring up and scale new heights, exposing one to a greater level of excellence. Which will it be for you?

If you have a disabled child, I would implore you to pay special attention towards him or her, because there may lie talents which most of the world have not witnessed, and which do not necessarily require them to be like other kids. Instead of following in sorrow, begin to work at helping them discover their gifts early on in life, nurture these gifts and you would be surprised at how adept they would become at the usage of these skills and will make you proud- yes, make you very proud.

Do not be so overcome by grief, that you fail to locate the gifts wrapped within your peculiar situation, you just might be sitting on a gold mine in form of ideas which would shake the world, or even something as a subtle painting which would pass across different beautiful messages all at once.

The beauty of not having what all others have is that there tends to be an inclination towards focus and more focus. This is one of the advantages of some disabilities- for example, the popular hymn writer- Keller, was blind; and so are a couple of other great musicians. Because of this, I would like to encourage Vasili to go in the line of these creative arts because they help one to connect deeply with their souls and inner personalities, and still, we are working on getting him to better communicate with additional aids.

We are really working hard to ensure that he is the best of himself, and attains the best with his situation, in life.

This is the spirit of hope being kept alive when the flames of hope are being put out on a daily basis. Situations, no matter how tough, should not break us but instead, they should make us.

Chapter 11:

Vasili's Future |

Vasili simply means 'King', and it is with awe that I have watched the complicated grandiose with which our son has lived his life.

The other day, I read about the story of a beautiful 15- year-old girl with Cerebral Palsy whose paintings have been selected for prestigious exhibitions and rivals the paintings of famous artists. Indeed, I feel a sense of satisfaction when I read such stories because the subtle implication is that there is a place for our children in the world today. I need not fret, only discover my boy's skills and hone them to a state of perfection so he can be a further inspiration to many, as this girl's story indeed inspires. For the time being, his inspiration and awareness of his tragedy has helped and will continue to help many more. Sadly, I would rather that he, and many others in his situation, had not had this story define him to help others, but selfishly I wish he had a simple life and one of the regular growing pains of children his age.

I've also read about people with Cerebral Palsy who went on to college, and later on became teachers, who got married and have been able to achieve all kinds of beautiful things. I hope Vasili gets to do so, and it would make our entire family happy. But even without, I know my son is severely disabled I am so proud of his resilience and strength, he makes us all so proud.

However, I am scared for him. I am scared of exposing him to the world especially when my wife or I are not here, or when we are too old to cope. If he gains some independence, or not, when we are not around, would there be children who are ever ready to pick on the weak ones, bully him? Would he be able to have a social life like his sister does? How will he incorporate living with his disability into a seemingly "normal" life? I wish he could go to the same school as his sisters, but he needs to attend a school where special educational needs are taken into consideration.

I sincerely prayed for him, that in the midst of it all, God would send people who would treat him with great respect across his way. Those who wouldn't agree that he should be treated super nicely, for they were the ones who could bring out the strength hidden in him. It was this set of people - caregivers, teachers, even strangers with good hearts maybe; but mostly caregivers together with us who would show him how capable he is and never accepting anything less than perfection from him.

They would register disappointment when they felt that way towards him, and radiate love and triumph when those were the emotions he deserved. With them, he would know that when he did well, he had really done well, and it wasn't an ego boost or a desire to help the disabled child feel good.

How about friends? I thought about if he would have real friends - the sort I had while growing up. I know that he would find friends in his sisters but what of outside the home? Would he find anyone who would love him enough to want to spend enough time with him, as opposed to other healthy children? Children had none of the cloaks of pretence that we older folks could readily put on, and when they loved it was pure, but would he find anyone to treat him in this way? I wasn't really expecting him to have any sleep-overs or to go to summer camps where he would have to spend the night elsewhere besides home, but I was at least hopeful that he would have one friend who could stay over at our house with him and with whom he can find some interests as he grows.

I have seen people with the same condition, who are adults and are doing quite fine, but I wonder how things would be for him then, how his sisters would treat him? I shouldn't be afraid that his sisters wouldn't treat him right, after all they do that amazingly perfectly now, but the doubts do come in at times. It's like it's with a particular wind from the east. But then, I get encouraged each time I see Vasili's encouraging smile.

As he grows, I seem to be concerned about his quality of life rather than him simply living life as he sees. Before, all I had just been grateful about was the fact that he was alive. But now, I think about more than that. Although, he often seems too wise for his age, I often sense questions emanating from him; like a lack of understanding of how different he seemed to be from every other person, why it took much more time to communicate with him, seeing that he was both deaf and blind. Questions almost flow from the abrupt turning of his head, when he seems to get what I am trying to pass across in terms of colours; and indeed, I am beginning to sense an artistic persona emanating from him.

I hope he would be able to channel some of the pain he has felt, and his pain gets really severe sometimes; into something really artistic or beautiful. We haven't found it completely yet, but I know that we will find that golden spot in our little Spartan, that spot which, if he fits into, is so perfect for him that the world stops to look at our boy who has fought through so many odds yet remains alive; defying all odds to stay strong. I can feel it deeply within me that he would tell his own story, through whatever means he chooses or discovers, but he would discover an outlet for all of this pain which he feels. I do not say this only because I love him, but because I can feel this vibe he emanates, one of strength that would not be silenced, no matter what, and would keep trudging on even in the face of innumerable dangers. I might not know it all, but I know that exciting days are sure to come concerning our little Spartan. I know that in years to come, all of these would be just like prophetic words because they would be so true, they would give life.

All we have to do is hold on tightly to our faith in him, showing him so much love regardless of failures, and actually allowing him to be himself. Refusing to project the fears which we have about him, on him; and allowing him the freedom of discovering all that lies within him and around him. Then he can approach the future with the confidence of one who might not know what gift is wrapped within that beautiful wrapping sheet, but knows that whatever it is, it would be beautiful. It would definitely be worth it, whenever it was time for it to be opened; and that time indeed, would unfold what was in store, for him.

Chapter 12:

Dealing with Guilt |

One of the facts, which took my wife and I a long time to get a hold of, was that Vasili's state wasn't our fault. It was hard to voice this for a really long time, because I think it haunted us both to think that we couldn't have prevented what had befallen him. What if we had taken him to the hospital immediately we noticed something was wrong without waiting for the midwife who had worsened everything for us?

My wife not only wondered about how Vasili's situation could have been prevented, but also repeatedly blamed herself for getting pregnant the third time. With an already disabled child, why did she allow herself to get pregnant? She would often wonder if it was all her fault. I wouldn't trivialise the effect of this guilt on both of us, as I also had my fair bit of it. I felt guilty for fathering my beautiful kids. I also felt guilty for sometimes switching off and not being there for them as I ought to at times. I felt very guilty for sometimes leaving Elena to handle all of the stress by herself when I just couldn't cope anymore. I cspecially felt guilty during those periods where I overate so much, became morbidly obese and wasn't of much use to myself, let alone any other person.

Each of us wallowed in guilt for a considerable time and it wasn't until we started going for counselling, and even in recent years making great friendships in personal development courses I felt I could learn from, that we really began to express these suppressed thoughts and finally accepted, after some more counselling sessions, that we weren't at fault. It had affected our relationship, strained what was left of our marriage so much that we had to work on building it over again from scratch, and this went on for quite a while. Particularly for Elena, it was relieving. It opened us up to a new level of love for our son and we were able to put most of our guilt aside. One way we have learnt to cope with this situation, is to simply open up and talk to each other, once feelings of guilt begin to pop up, and usually, the other person is able to clear up perspectives, and thus we help to raise each other's spirits. We have learnt how much communication can be of help to our emotional health, and how easily we can get those feelings when we talk to each other about it. At such moments, I usually reflect on how lucky I am to have someone who loves me and whom I love, someone whom I can talk to about these feelings and who totally understands me. Elena is my personal blessing from God. One which I never wish to lose and which I do not take for granted in any way.

And certainly, our unity has helped us immensely. It has helped through all of the different tests and evaluations, through all of the different surgeries and through all of the pain we feel our son experiencing. Standing strongly together has enabled us to overcome those challenging moments because each of us knows that we have each other's full support.

While many may not have learnt to be grateful for all that they have, our state as a family has helped us to be more grateful each and every time we see an even subtle improvement, and I find this to be particularly helpful for us when we are faced with guilt.

If you are in a similar situation or anything which guilt trips you, I would advise you to either talk to someone about it, or to see a counsellor. Meanwhile, right now, I would also ask you to stop blaming yourself or feeling terrible because of what you think you have done or not done. Also, I would implore couples to work hand in hand, not to blame the other party for anything, especially because in situations such as this, words are more hurtful and might create such a gap or a breach in communication that it becomes almost impossible to reconcile the differences and come together as a couple once again. At this juncture, regardless of what you may think as individuals, you sorely need each other. One cannot survive without the other and the most pertinent relationship that you would need at these trying moments is the relationship of your spouse or partner. As this is a shared grief, you both can better relate your inner feelings of guilt with one another without expecting judgment, but rather expecting support to triumph over it all. This is because for us, Elena and me, unity, I must confess, has been one of the most important factors that have helped us get this far in our sojourn, and through all of the pain which we have experienced.

I know how it feels, and how many years it took us to get to this stage (and we are still in the process of learning this, every day), so I understand that you might want to take your time to nurse yourself back to health.

Take that time and allow yourself to grow out of that feeling of guilt. Never forget the fact that you feel guilty doesn't necessarily mean you are guilty; something just happened beyond your control to someone you assumed you had protection over and who trusts you enough to give you freely some rights in their lives, and you feel you've failed them. Not so; for some events, we cannot control. You might have to remind yourself over and over again that you couldn't have pre-empted this situation and that if you could, you would have done something to prevent it, but never accept that something which was beyond your control, was your fault. Daily remind yourself that if you had even the slightest inkling of what the situation at the time portended, that you would not have allowed it to go that far. Relish in the love that you have for that child. Let it guide you to recovery, knowing that the fact you loved him or her would not have permitted you to let anything untoward happen to them. This was a happenstance, one that caught you and everyone around who loved him or her, unawares. I have had several conversations with myself, where I have had to remind myself that I could not have pre-empted Vasili's condition, and so, I could not have prevented it. Therefore, I am not at fault. This has helped me to be able to show him as much love as I possibly can. It's beautiful how much freedom you have when you don't feel guilty.

Sometimes when someone who has walked or who is walking the road you are on, says something like this, you should listen because there is, embedded in them, a lifetime of experiences, of falling flat on their faces and standing up, of living in regret and deciding to come out of it to live a truly beautifully designed life.

138

When next those feelings of guilt begin to rise up within you, do not let them fester or grow into something huge. No! Nip those feelings right in the bud. Refuse to let those thoughts linger, or to allow yourself to become so discouraged that you become unable to do anything productive. Instead of wallowing in that guilt, if possible, find someone else whom your story can inspire. Do something productive, make yourself useful. I say this because another way in which guilt can manifest is, as you are feeling that doing any other thing besides taking care of your child or loved one is sacrilegious. I know, because this is one area which my wife and I had to deal with guilt for a very long time. We sometimes felt as though if we had any time to ourselves for fun, we were doing injustice to the children. And this was hinged on the fact that we were at fault for their situation, which of course, wasn't true. When we were able to get over the feeling of guilt that we were at fault, we were then able to face it squarely, the other feeling of guilt, that we couldn't do anything for fun - in effect, that our lives had to be over.

Think about it this way: do you think your child would want you to perpetually live in sadness? Do you think your child or other family members whom you are taking care of would like to hear about you years from now, and know that you were completely unproductive because of them? How much of your life have you already wasted feeling guilty, and how many more do you plan to waste languishing in guilt? The terrible thing about guilt is that it is non-progressive and can never lead to anything good. It can only end up in more and more feelings of guilt. Years from now, if you choose to keep on feeling guilty, you would look back with even more regrets. So what are my suggestions? Take a last look at those matters which you have chronically languished in guilt. This is the very last look you would be giving them, so I suggest that you take as much time as you would like to.

Have you done so? Good. It's time to say bye to your guilt and to move on. It's time to progress and leave this baggage behind you. It's time for goodbye.

Say your byes respectfully.

Chapter 13:

On Acceptance and Day-To-Day Living |

It certainly isn't easy to take care of children, especially as sometimes they act way too fast and they are always in a state of constant activity, jumping here and there. Although, ironically, we only had this experience with our eldest child, while the other two tend to be a little more challenging. And so, life on a daily basis hasn't been so effortless.

Instead, it is filled with days that seem tiring even at 5 in the morning when you consider the sheer amount of energy it would take for your child to be awakened, bathed, dressed and fed. That alone, is enough work for the day, and coupled with a full-term job and ensuring the house is neat, it's pretty much more than a full day's work in fact. I sometimes wishfully think that the powers that be should have allotted more time than 24hours for those of us with disabled Spartans.

However, there is one thing which I would like to say and especially right on the heels of dealing with guilt.

When you have finally eased into the role of someone who really has to care for a disabled individual, you would find that it's extremely difficult for you to have sweet rest. And if you do have the opportunity to rest, you are quick to let resting go to someone else who has 'less work on their hands' than to allow your tired body to rest. But here is my sincere advice: When you have the opportunity to rest or relax, kindly do so; not only for yourself but for that Spartan who has been placed in your care, more for the sake of the maintenance of such a healthy state of mind that you can then transfer onto him or her. It only takes one who is in a great state of good health to fully impact positively in the life of the other he is caring for, you don't want to break and let your Spartan try to find ways to take care of themselves (that is even totally out of the question) or do you want to become an extra burden on whomever you may re-quire at the time to help with the care of your loved one? I know it may seem a little selfish at the time but trust me, it's your mind playing tricks on you... there is absolutely nothing selfish about your actions and it would only serve to help you and your Spartan get the best care that you both need.

Resting is not to be seen as being inconsiderate, as you may be tempted to feel. Sometimes, you just need to act on that directive to zone out, to focus on you and you alone. Yes, it might indeed be difficult for you to accept it at this time but know that getting a good night rest might seem to make you less industrious but instead it is making more productive. Decide early on, that whenever you can get some time off to get yourself in the right frame of mind, that you will not pass the opportunity but will fully harness it.

For me, with my additional Vitamin B12 deficiency, I find it incredibly difficult on some days to even get out of bed due to the incessant headaches which I can't seem to stop having. I had stopped taking my injections a few months ago because I

142

was told to, or rather was made to believe that it was okay to stop getting the injections after a few years, when it apparently wasn't okay, and well, the after-effects are a killer. I have recently resumed taking the injections, but I still have pain and there are days when the pain is almost paralysing.

Because I am sometimes divided between ensuring I am okay and that my kids are fine, it sometimes takes a lot for me to do it all, and do it well. Whenever I can, I take care of my kids but whenever I am struggling, I choose to look on the brighter side and ensure that I am upbeat so that I can take care of them even better.

One valid point which I am trying to share is, that we should accept our current states, and with much gusto, proceed to developing our strengths to cope with whatever it is that we have been given to handle. This is the focal point of present existence, to get as much positive and even where necessary make the negatives work in our favour. It will do us a whole lot of good as it would those whose care have been entrusted to us.

In all, as always, there is joy even in our pain!

Chapter 14:

The Spartan Within Each of Us |

The definition of the word Spartan, which I hold very close to my heart, is that it means to be 'Courageous in the face of pain, danger or adversity'. I couldn't get a better term to summarise who Vasili, my king is, and the kind of personality which he possesses. Sometimes, I think, that he must possess some sort of super human powers to be able to survive all of his daily battles. Although I might complain about our lives as members of a family and how all of this affects us, he is the one who is really affected. Our emotional trauma cannot be compared to the traumatic experiences of a 5-year-old who is condemned to live life within his own prison which only happens to lack handcuffs. On second thought, it could be considered that he has restrictions far greater than just a pair of handcuffs...

Yet, he maintains such strength that I am consistently amazed by how far he has come. But somehow, I know that this strength was born out of the sheer will to survive a crazy situation. One in which a lack of such will would condemn you to death and you had to choose to either keep fighting, or to die. There weren't that many options, and you just had to choose one.

I have found out that there's only one way to get on in life, only one way by which you can truly move on and surmount every kind of obstacle that you might be presented with. Only one. What is this magical way which helps us to cope in spite of all odds? This is it: find the Spartan within you and pursue your goals relentlessly. Pursue your aspirations, your dreams, in spite of whatever problem presents itself to you. I am eternally grateful to Vasili for showing me that indeed, it is possible to move on and to achieve great feats in life regardless of how many problems are in your way.

As little as my Spartan is, I have seen him try to walk, fall severely, and yet get back up on his feet. When he wants to do something, he puts his all into it and tries his best to achieve his goals. He works so hard on himself, demonstrating patience and persistence. He has forged great relationships with his little peers, care workers and his therapists and expresses himself in his cheeky, humorous manner making it such a delight to witness. Such stamina; I can only admire.

The unveiling of the Spartan within you might help you cope with disability, beat cancer, kick other chronic illnesses [to touch?]. Smile through all forms of unimaginable pain, take care of, with a hearty attitude, someone who is ill or hurt; whatever your Spartan helps you to do, it is unique to you. Each Spartan is individual, strong in his/her own way and determined to see and make the best out of every situation. Might you determine to hold on to your Spartan, you would discover such an enriched life and begin to count your troubles as blessings. A certain light would be cast on those seemingly unfortunate incidents and you would count them as the harbingers of great things to come.

Our little Spartan has given us hope and not just that, he has helped us to carefully unwrap our very own Spartans within, and to come out with a deeply rooted, unshaken knowledge and belief that we can come out of any challenging situation positive and smiling. Apart from learning a lot from him, we have become interested in gathering information and being articulate. We have read books, watched videos, listened to audio notes, all in the bid to know more; just so we can live a harmonised life as a family. From these experiences and life lessons, we have grown to love more in our marriage, grown to love and treat our children fairly and rightly, and definitely grown to deal with different kinds of children and people around us.

Also, the specific virtues and behavioural methods learnt from this cannot be overemphasised. Our disposition is now so great that our friends and family members attest to it. They say that truly, the addition of Vasili to the family has been very much more of a blessing. Our reactions and response to stimuli have been adjusted to bring about beautiful relationships and a great sort of networking.

Truly, having the privilege of being Vasili's father has helped me to grow as a person. Within the last year, I can proudly say that I have evolved into a new version of me. Reflecting upon my son's journey has helped me to go on a journey into personal development, into growing to become all that I was destined to be in my own personal life. In lieu of this, my business has taken on a new face within the last year, having the much-needed daily dose of inspiration from my son who helps me see the good in every situation. My business has taken on a new look, and unlike the old me who is

147

quick to quit at any sign of pressure or at any problematic situation, I have found that the strength and resilience which I have developed while nursing Vasili has immensely helped me to stay and face my battles squarely. I have learnt how to talk back at those situations and keep on facing them head on until I attain victory. Who would have thought I could do this? I wouldn't. This has made my business boom, and for those who had known me previously, they now see a new person who doesn't get moved by circumstances and who would rather wait until he wins.

Through the inspiration of all my children and my wife, I am gradually becoming a person who to myself at least, is known as a winner. To me, that is definitely inspiring.

Not only that but in business, I have also learnt the act of compassion. Whilst it may seem almost impossible for a businessman or woman to have this trait, and instead to only consider monetary compensation, I have found the ability to be firm yet compassionate, for these two qualities don't have to be mutually exclusive. I would gladly attribute this to having to be very compassionate in the care of our son, in such a way that we can make firm decisions as regards his care, yet still love him enough to show our depth of sensitivity.

You should see his eyes and how bright his smile is. Our little Spartan has helped us to note the importance of something as seemingly little as a smile, to hold onto what could be deemed as an out of place grin and to understand the true value of human communication and bodily touch. Indeed, we have become stronger, but also our capacity to love has greatly increased. As with each new challenge, we have had to find a

148

place to love even more. We love him, we care for him, we choose to help him see his own strength as he grows up. We choose to encourage him along whichever paths he chooses to tread, and we choose ultimately, to never, ever give up on him. This is for Vasili; our little Spartan.

This is for the one who has inspired us to grow up into mature beings and into people who are able to love relentlessly, every day. For Vasili, the one whose love shines brightly through his eyes and whom, even when silent, quietly teaches us such virtues as compassion, love, patience, forbearance and strength. I consider myself favoured to be a parent to such a formidable child, for most of the time, he isn't the one who learns from me - it's the other way around. I end up most times learning from him and drawing strength just from watching him live such an inspirational life. On the basis of this inspiration of which I am fortunate to tap into on a daily basis, I want to inspire you never to give up, and always to stay hopeful regardless of what comes your way. As commonly quoted, when life gives you lemons, you can make lemonade. Instead of looking at all the negative connotations of whatever state you are in, find it within you to locate the positivity of such a situation and work towards becoming the best possible version of yourself. Just as my wife and I have found purpose in the pain which we have experienced, I strongly believe that you can find purpose in any pain which you are also experiencing. I strongly believe that whatever doesn't kill you will only make you stronger, if you will let it.

I strongly believe that you have a Spartan within yourself, waiting to be unleashed and desirous of showing the world how strong you truly are.

Don't fret, instead, let yourself see how much joy can be found in your pain, and don't be surprised if you stumble upon such rich lessons that you end up being grateful for that pain.

Chapter 15:

Blue Notes |

I have decided to create a brief summary of a check list and things to look out for and do to help you and your loved one cope with the challenges of disability. This is actually a product of research and my desire to want to help as many families going through the same challenges as we have had and still are going through. To take these few steps as they have been helpful for us, to also make them work for you. They are not exhaustive and are only a reflection of my thoughts being one who has had extensive experience managing two children with disabilities.

Some of these I may have spoken about in the body of these texts but I am only writing them out to help give clear insight as to what to expect and how to react to ensure that you get the best out of the present situation. In all of these, I am learning as well and would also take away a few things from this page.

Recognise that you are not alone

You are not alone in this, never for once feel that way. I would examine some of the emotions that you may experience in the beginning phase or you may be experiencing now, and I would want you to know that your case is not isolated. The feeling of isolation at the time of diagnosis is almost universal among parents. You are a part of a larger community of people with shared grief and you can take advantage of that community, to find the required strength to carry on and make good a life so beautiful that it becomes worthy of emulation.

In this book, there are many recommendations to help you handle feelings of separation and isolation. It helps to know that these feelings have been experienced by many, many others, that understanding and constructive help are available to you and your child, and that you are not alone.

Guilt

"Did I do something to cause this? Am I being punished for something I have done? Did I take care of myself when I was pregnant? Did my wife take good enough care of herself when she was pregnant?" There are usually so many questions that would run through your mind and like it was for me at the beginning. As I have told you, there was so much self-reproach and remorse that could only come from feeling guilty for something I most certainly wasn't responsible for, and yes, I may have been able to change a few things if given back that time, but I can't get it back. So today I have to live positively for myself and my family, they need me to be in great shape and falling into guilt would be for them, a disservice.

Guilt feelings may also be manifested in spiritual and religious interpretations and misinterpretations of blame and punishment. When your child cries or seem to be in pain, there is this feeling of "Why me?" or "Why my child?" Some other parents may resort to the spiritual and ask questions as "Why has

God done this to me?" Oftentimes we raised our eyes towards the sky asking: "What did I ever do to deserve this?" For me, it was to also go to somewhere isolated and scream at particularly no one to release my pent-up emotions. I was always asking questions that most certainly I had no answers to, even when Elena and I would sometimes take breaks, there was this nagging feeling of guilt, whispering silently into our soul, trying hard to make us feel that we were doing something really bad to be relaxed whilst our child was in such a condition. It wasn't easy at first to shake off these feelings, but as we began to open up with each other and explored the option of dialoguing, sharing our pain and supposed guilt, it became easier for us to rise above it. And today, though, I can't say that we are out of the woods, but we are getting there, one day at a time.

Confusion

Confusion is also one of the states you and your spouse may find yourselves in during this traumatic period. This stems from the fact that you most probably are not fully aware, nor do you have a full understanding of what is happening and what is most likely to happen. You will find yourself having sleepless nights worrying about what was to come, bouts of confusion and uncertainty. In this period, there may be information overload. Or, as in our case, the hoarding of information. There will be so many new medical words thrown at you, words you would almost have no business with if not for the challenge you have found yourself in, but please make the most of it. Do not let the situation overwhelm you, find that inner peace. I know it may sound a little difficult at the time, but it will help you to make sense of it all.

Hopelessness

When it seems that the feeling of confusion is waning, you may now have to grapple with that feeling of not being able to change the situation that has bedevilled your child. For some, they have spoken of how hopeless they felt in the face of the problem, but I just want you to understand that you cannot change the fact that your child has a disability, and that acceptance takes time. I understand that you want to feel competent and capable of handling their own life situations, but the peculiarity of the situation would force them to rely on the judgments, opinions, and recommendations of others; many of whom you have no prior relationship with nor a bond of trust. It is okay to feel hopeless, but what's not okay, is to stay that way. Seek out support groups, find comfort in one another, understand that the situation may seem hopeless now, but that's not the way it is going to remain. Like I have said earlier, search for information on the ailment and work closely with the doctors so that you are aware of the treatments and interventions that are being carried out, that way you can build trust in their ability to care for your loved one.

Rejection

Some parents may face rejection, as for Elena and me, there were times we felt so alone; together and sometimes individually. Even quite early on in Vasili's prognosis, I couldn't bring myself to understand why the hospital staff treated us as outcasts, no one was speaking to us and even when they spoke to one another around us, it was in hushed tones. This bothered me, but over time, I was to overcome it. During this period of time when so many different feelings can flood the mind and heart, there is no way to measure how intensely a parent may experience this constellation of emotions.

Not all parents go through these phases, but it is important for parents to identify with all of the potentially troublesome feelings that can arise so that they will know that they are not alone. There are quite a number of constructive actions that you can take immediately, that would offer relieve to you some-what, as there are many sources of help, communication, and reassurance. Do not take lightly the importance of finding help, you will need it.

Join a Support Group

There is a countless number of support groups you can become a part of. I have earlier told of how Elena and I had to pay for support. Though the therapy did a lot of good, the most good was done when I was able to connect with parents who had the same challenges and together, were providing support to each other. The beauty of it all is that in this sphere, there is no shame, there is no need to want to fit in, in many ways, we are all broken and needing help. Such help can come from us sharing our experiences and also offering solutions to some of the nagging issues that we may encounter as we go on this destined path. The groups also serve as a source of inspiration because you get to listen to soul uplifting testimonies of children who have overcome the boundaries that medical science have set for them. These stories help to lift your faith and give you hope for a new and better tomorrow. It also avails you the opportunity to come to the awareness of the rich, innate abilities that exist inside of your loved one, waiting to be harnessed and unleashed on the world.

The groups are a great place to find yourself and you can find them on social media as well as local charities.

Take One Day at a Time

Fears of the future can cause you to relapse into a shell that may be difficult to come out of. Living with the reality of the here and now can help better manage all the nagging questions of "what if's" of the future. Although it may not seem possible at the beginning, good things will definitely come to you. Beautiful moments would be created with your bundle of joy, it is best to relish the moments and to continue to allow the positives to have a place in your life. Worrying about the future will only deplete your limited resources. You have enough to focus on; get through each day, one step at a time and please do make sure that you try to enjoy it to the fullest as you go along.

Learn the Terminology

When you are introduced to new terminology, you should not be hesitant to ask what it means. Whenever someone uses a word that you don't understand, stop the conversation for a minute and ask the person to explain the word, this is in continuation of your learning.

Seek Information

Some parents seek virtually tons of information; others are not so persistent. The important thing is that you request accurate information. Don't be afraid to ask questions, because asking questions will be your first step in beginning to understand more about your child and the condition.

I sought to learn all I could about Kernicterus and Cerebral Palsy, after I had made the decision to take control of my life and be the best for my king. I asked questions and ensured that I acquainted myself with the medical process that Vasili had to undergo. This helped me to better understand the condition and to also seek ways to help him become better. I found ways to help with his physiotherapy by learning some massage techniques that were beneficial to his wellbeing. Not only did it save us some money on bills but it also brought me closer to him; it created between us, a bond that has led me on a path of recovery and true self-actualization and one for which I am eternally grateful.

Learn to ask the right questions, and always remember to request copies of evaluations, diagnostic reports, and progress reports.

Do Not Be Intimidated

It is okay to sometimes feel inadequate but as you progress, you may have to stand up to a few people, particularly those in the medical or educational professions. Don't be intimidated by their credentials. What is of the uppermost importance to you, is the welfare of your child. But please express your opinions and or disaffection in a courteous manner. Do not be daunted by the educational backgrounds of these and other personnel who may be involved in treating or helping your child. You do not have to apologise for wanting to know what is happening. Do not be concerned that you are being a bother or are asking too many questions. Remember, this is your child, and the situation has a profound effect on your life and on your child's future. Therefore, it is important that you learn as much as you can about your situation. Also, don't allow people to treat you anyhow. I mean, if they misbehave, don't let it get to you, please. If you are down, it would reflect on the child, which we both know is never good.

People start being rude to you when you are blocking their way in the queue, in a public place, while trying to help your child up, they don't care that you are struggling so they tut or frown when you bumped into them. It's crazy, really. You just have to wonder at times if some people these days have lost humanity and any empathy. We can only pity them that they are uneducated and so disrespectful through lack of ignorance to our form of hardships.

Saying this you will also meet such compassionate, helpful people who are really willing to help. We have been blessed to have had much more kindness than the negative, thank goodness!

Do Not Be Afraid to Show Emotion

I was like this, but it could only last for a while. A lot of parents feel it's not right to display emotions; it is understandable that you are hurt by the turn of events so it's okay to cry. Don't repress your emotions because you believe it to be a sign of weakness or not wanting to let people know how you are feeling. The strongest fathers of children with disabilities whom I know, are not afraid to show their emotions. They understand that revealing feelings does not diminish a person's strength.

At the beginning, I was not happy with all the pity that people had on their faces whenever they saw Vasili or asked about him. One time, I blurted out and said things I shouldn't have said to one of my colleagues. He was in the habit of giving me the sorry nod, and pat on the back whenever I mentioned Vasili. When I noticed it, I smartly made mention of it that I was fine with my son's condition, even though I wasn't, no one would be, they only accept and live with it. He responded that he was only trying to look out for him but I made him understand that it left a hole in my heart as it made me feel that my son was an invalid and that I was less of a father. He had laughed it off but he never did it again.

I have learnt that it is just good and healthy to let your emotions out. People struggle with words to say to even try to comprehend what you are going through, especially when you are in a grieving process so bottling up would only compound the very issue before you, it's like a time bomb waiting to explode. It's okay to break down at times. No one is saying that you should be a crying puppet or become a show prince or drama queen, you only have to stop acting strong when you really are not. Let the pain show. At times there's an easiness that comes from it, and I speak from experience. A lot of fathers at some of the forums we are a part of, such as PICK (Parents with Infants and Children with Kernicterus) have learnt that I am very expressive in sharing my thoughts and always there to help and support newcomers. There is no need to hold up a facade.

Learn to Deal with Natural Feelings of Bitterness and Anger

Feelings of bitterness and anger are inevitable when you realise that you must revise the hopes and dreams you originally had for your child. Even more so as with our case when you know that the damage would have been averted if only someone had taken a little time to just do what was right.

It is very important that you recognise your anger, feel it, and then learn to let it go. Sometimes it could seem like a herculean task and if it feels so, it is okay to seek outside help to do this. It may not feel like it, but life will get better and the day will come when you will feel positive again. By acknowledging and working through your negative feelings, you will become better equipped to meet new challenges, and to help and support your loved ones. Forgiveness is never easy. But in the end, you will be the person to most benefit from it. Anger drains your energy and initiative and is like a slow poison festering in your body.

Maintain a Positive Outlook

A positive attitude will be one of the genuinely valuable tools for dealing with problems. There is, truly, always a positive side to whatever is happening. For example, when Vasili was found to have Kernicterus, in spite of the challenges and the realisation that all of this could have been avoided, I had to let go of all of the hurt and focus more on the strength that shone from his face every day. I drew strength from him and focused more on making every day and every experience count.

160

For me, that has been the hallmark of my new existence. This also has a multiplier effect on Elena as she is, by the day, looking more beautiful and radiant.

Keep in Touch with Reality

To stay in touch with reality is to accept life the way it is. To stay in touch with reality is also to recognise that there are some things that we can change and other things that we cannot change. The task for all of us is learning which things we can change and then set about doing that.

Remember That Time Is on Your Side

Time heals many wounds. This does not mean that living with and raising a child who has problems will be easy, but it is fair to say that, as time passes, a great deal can be done to alleviate the problem. Therefore, time does help.

Find Programmes for Your Child

Do not, for any reason, allow your fear to take over you. I understand that you may feel the need to protect them like I would always for Vasili, but I understand better now that they need to be out and engage in as much physical activity as their energy can take. They adapt better and it helps them build social skills. For Vasili, in spite of his peculiar situation, still would benefit from such engagement. While finding programmes for your child with a disability, keep in mind that programmes are also available for the rest of your family.

Take Care of Yourself

Get sufficient rest; eat as well as you can; take time for yourself; reach out to others for emotional support, avoid pity in whatever form, whether it is self-pity or pity from others, pity is not what you want. Empathy yes, but not pity.

Decide How to Deal with Others

During this period, you may feel saddened by or angry about the way people are reacting to you or your child. Many people's reactions to serious problems are caused by a lack of understanding; simply not knowing what to say, or fear of the unknown. Understand that many people don't know how to behave when they see a child with differences, and so they may react inappropriately. Think about and decide how you want to deal with stares or questions. Try not to use too much energy being concerned about people who are not able to respond in ways you might prefer, instead educate those who show an interest.

Remember that this is Your Child

This person is your child, first and foremost. Granted, your child's development may be different from that of other children, but this does not make your child less valuable, less human, less important, or in less need of your love and parenting. Love and enjoy your child. The child comes first; the disability comes second. If you can relax and take the positive steps just outlined, one at a time, you will do the best you can, your child will benefit, and you can look forward to the future with hope.

A Collection of Poems

Trust me I have never been a poet, or have I ever had the nerve to even attempt to be. Faced with happy times but also with painful times, the heart leads the head and I found myself writing off the cuff poems. I thought I would share some here with you. Each poem was born at different stages of our journey, so some will relate to certain areas of this book.

This chapter is dedicated to some of the most amazing people in my life. The first poem is for Vasili, and I attempt to write from his perspective, to write what he would have loved to write down if he could hold a pen to paper, to feel his pain and to put myself in his well-worn, five-year-old shoes. I might fall short, but the major thing is, that I tried.

The second poem is for my rock, my Elena. The one whose womb birthed this king and has produced three beautiful children whom I can indeed call God's blessings upon our lives. It wouldn't be out of place for me to call her my blessing for that is what she has been to me. Through the thick and thin, for better or for worse, she has stood by me these fourteen years and I am very grateful that I got the chance to live life with her.

I hope you enjoy my attempt at poetry.

For Vasili

Senses

Alone, I feel at times, my heart aches with fear.

My own cries of pain that even I struggle to hear.

I may have less body senses, but I am far from lost.

I can sense real people's love and those with hearts of frost.

It's easy to ignore me as I may look lost and contorted.

Some people feel my disability is a burden, a life that's unsorted.

Listen to me intensely as I share something I know.

'Sshhh!' don't tell everybody my communications are starting to show.

And as I morph into someone I will be proud of, I tell you a secret of something I've learnt.

I will tell you how I feel, don't worry; my bridges won't be burnt.

There is no need to judge or dislike those who mock me; it's not how I roll.

I will just watch you quietly and I'll listen to your soul.

One day, you will realise something really special, something only I know.

When you face life's hardships, this secret will show.

Keep swimming hard, the choppy waters are deep.

And when you reach the land, the gradient is steep.

Keep in your mind that boy that you know;

Whilst your wading through that deep hard snow.

I won't be here forever, so don't forget what I want you to see. I'm a Spartan! That's what my daddy calls me.

I just want to help others. That is all my legacy can be.

Keep loving each other and keep me in your mind.

Don't complain; get on with it, do not allow yourself to go blind.

For Elena

My love to you excites me in a way I find difficult to show.

With big hurdles that seem impossible to clear!

Our struggles entwined, they become clearer year by year.

Effusive by nature, our dreams were being left behind.

I am doing my best to strive forward with the end in mind.

Let me express where I am striving to go:

A place where I can help my family and myself grow.

Yes, knowledge is power but let's not forget that the heart is the king.

You taught me that, the day I gave you your ring.

Like children when we first met, our dreams altogether seemed so big!

Then one day all broken, stepped on so easily just like a broken twig.

But let's not forget, that the tree is still growing tall and strong.

There will be situations that hold us back, but for us, no, not for long!

This enduring tree has felt many hard seasons, and it certainly shows.

Witnessed by the scars that bare all the tormented throws.

Through the hard winds, I now have faith our roots will never let go!

From years of tormented seasons through the seasons and cold, cold snow.

We grow stronger together each year we grow, grow, grow

If you look closely this tree is two trees joined and our roots entwined forever

This is our true secret that keeps us together.

Disabled, but still growing, and nothing can stop us now.

Our strength and lessons learned what can I say; wow, just wow!

The secret taught by hardships that no course can ever teach.

A deep understanding that together we have much further reach.

Yes; our little Spartan has taught us much through an ordeal that's hard to fathom.

But with great loss we have been on a journey, with a future that will no doubt blossom.

So thank you my dear wife, for helping me grow.

You're ever so kind and you let me grow with the people I trust and know.

For you're my dearest foundation, my dream, and I will never let go.

What an amazing woman whose heart holds no hate!

A great wife, a fantastic mother, and my dearest soul mate.

Here is a poem which is commonly known but it really resonated with me at such difficult times....

Welcome to Holland

I am often asked to describe the experience of raising a child with a disability - to try to help people who have not shared that unique experience to understand it, to imagine how it would feel. It's like this......

When you're going to have a baby, it's like planning a fabulous vacation trip - to Italy. You buy a bunch of guide books and make your wonderful plans. The Coliseum. The Michelangelo David. The gondolas in Venice. You may learn some handy phrases in Italian. It's all very exciting.

After months of eager anticipation, the day finally arrives. You pack your bags and off you go. Several hours later, the plane lands. The stewardess comes in and says, "Welcome to Holland."

"Holland?!?" you say. "What do you mean Holland??

I signed up for Italy! I'm supposed to be in Italy. All my life I've dreamed of going to Italy."

But there's been a change in the flight plan. They've landed in Holland and there you must stay.

The important thing is that they haven't taken you to a horrible, disgusting, filthy place, full of pestilence, famine and disease. It's just a different place.

So you must go out and buy new guide books. And you must learn a whole new language. And you will meet a whole new group of people you would never have met.

It's just a different place. It's slower-paced than Italy, less flashy than Italy. But after you've been there for a while and you catch your breath, you look around.... and you begin to notice that Holland has

Wind mills....and Holland has tulips. Holland even has Rembrandts.

But everyone you know is busy coming and going from Italy... and they're all bragging about what a wonderful time they had there. And for the rest of your life, you will say "Yes, that's where I was supposed to go. That's what I had planned."

And the pain of that will never, ever, ever, ever go away... because the loss of that dream is a very, very, significant loss. But...if you spend your life mourning the fact that you didn't get to Italy, you may never be free to enjoy the very special, the very lovely things ... about Holland.

Epilogue

When you have been through as much in life as I have been privileged to go through within my relatively few years, you come to appreciate everything beautiful, and cherish small but notable fragments of joy.

Over and over again, I have had to ask myself why I had to go through all of this, if it had really been necessary. But in more recent times, I have learnt to count my blessings - to release the Spartan within myself, and the more I look at Vasili, the more I have learnt to do just this.

Writing this book brought tears to my eyes, seeing as I had to go through some of those emotions experienced within the past 5 years over and over again, and I hope indeed, that someone who is going through turbulent times would be blessed by some of the things I have documented in here.

It is my hope that no one would ever have to experience the amount of pain my family and I have been through these few years, but if you do go through some pain, I hope, that you would remember to release the Spartan within you to exhibit the courage which you truly possess.

Thank you for reading.

Acknowledgements

We would like to acknowledge and thank many people who have joined us on our journey. Some are mentioned in this book but there are many more people, friends and family and support groups that have helped along our journey. We as a family would like to say from the bottom of our heart. We love you and thank you.

27121399R00102

Made in the USA
Columbia, SC
25 September 2018